Discovering Your Divine Assignment

Robin Chaddock

HARVEST HOUSE PUBLISHERS

EUGENE, OREGON

Cover and interior design by Harvest House Publishers, Inc., Corey Fisher, designer

Cover photo © Comstock Images

DISCOVERING YOUR DIVINE ASSIGNMENT
Copyright © 2005 by Robin Chaddock
Published by Harvest House Publishers
Eugene, Oregon 97402
www.harvesthousepublishers.com

Library of Congress Cataloging-in-Publication Data
Chaddock, Robin.
  Discovering your divine assignment / Robin Chaddock.
    p. cm.
  Includes bibliographical references.
  ISBN 10: 0-7369-1576-1 (pbk.)
  ISBN 13: 978-0-7369-1576-2 (pbk.)
  1. Vocation—Christianity. 2. Christian life. I. Title.
  BV4740.C43 2005
  248.4—dc22   2005001506

Lovingly dedicated to all who have walked this path with me already. I have learned so much from each of you. And dedicated to all who are joining us. Joy in the journey.

He who was seated on the throne said,
"I am making everything new!"

REVELATION 21:5

Acknowledgments

I am deeply indebted to everyone who has made contributions to this book by sharing his or her thoughts and experiences. Many thanks to Paul Bird, Catherine Carvey, Kelly Charlier, Nancy Estabrook, Linda Forler, Julie Green, Marilyn Hillis, Tami Holland, Kaylus Horten, Sara Johnson, Evelyn Kaufman, Gerald Kaufman, Theresa Leibold, Jennifer Lipinski, Rani Moodley, Claudia Pierson, Michele Reel, MaryAnn Ruegger, Libby Sandstrom, Scott Sandstrom, and Jody Token.

"My Shelbyville group" worked through so much of this material with me, giving me feedback, helping fine-tune questions, and continually surprising me with their answers. Kudos to Camille Coers, Jeaneen Falconer, Sharon Orem, Mary Rinehart, Carolyn Statler, Dawn Whitfield, and Nancy Willis. I am grateful.

Many thanks to those who shared their stories. A good book is actually a community project, and I am delighted and grateful to be in community with you.

There are so many remarkable thinkers and doers who have gone before me in this whole area of call, mission, and purpose. I feel this book is just a continuation of the conversation we're all having all the time. Special thanks to Laurie Beth Jones and her work *The Path*. She has made foundational contributions to my life personally and professionally.

My family continues to amaze me in their good-humored acceptance of the writing life that engages me (sometimes to the exclusion of clean socks, a stocked refrigerator, and—this year—Christmas itself!). My husband, David, is an insightful sounding board, an ever-present parent, and a great hugger! My kids, Maddie and Grant, keep me humble and make me laugh. And my parents, Walt and Lenore, fill more gaps in our family life than they ever counted on when they moved closer to us. Thank you, dear ones, for giving me all of this and so much more!

I am again deeply grateful to my wonderful editor who, in this third book together, has also moved into the role of faithful encourager and compassionate sister in Christ. Thank you, Barb, for all of the support and honesty and companionship. You are a true professional as well as a delightful friend. I am thankful every day for the gracious gift of my relationship with Harvest House Publishers.

Finally, and at the end of the day, I am ever in awe of the love my Creator has for me and for his gracious gift of patience with me as I discovered my Divine Assignment and how to best use my life—and ultimately came to realize that what truly makes me happy is him.

CONTENTS

Introduction

❧

Tell me, what do you plan to do
with your one wild and precious life?

Mary Oliver

*I*f you had the chance to sit down face-to-face with God while you were still living on earth and ask him any question you wanted to, chances are excellent you would ask a question of your purpose: Why am I here? What do you want me to do with my life? Am I on the right track for living in your purpose for me? What in the world made you think I could do the things you're asking me to do? But you don't have to wait for a face-to-face meeting. You can ask God *now!* Are you in one of these places?

- You want to lay a good foundation for the choices you are making in career, relationships, and life expenditures.

- You have a nagging sense, as Stephen Covey put it, that you have been climbing the ladder of success only to discover it's propped up against the wrong wall.

- You are in a stagnant place where life is going along perhaps as planned, but it lacks depth, meaning, or a true reason to get out of bed.

- You have a good sense about your gifts and interests, but you just don't have the foundational "why?" in place yet.

- You have come to this point in your life through a transition that has left you wondering who you are and why you are on the planet.

- You are cut from the bolt of cloth that says, "Whatever will provide me a closer, deeper relationship with God—bring it on!"

Now is the time to discover your God-given purpose—your Divine Assignment.

"Purpose" Isn't What You Think

When most of us think of purpose, we think of something we intend to do or accomplish. We see purpose as activity based—something we can point to and say, "I did that." Yet a life based on activity and accomplishments has left many of us restless and searching for something more. When jobs change or family responsibilities are altered, we cast about looking for a new purpose, a new reason for living. When things don't turn out as we planned, does that mean we missed our purpose or we no longer have one?

Not if we realize that purpose is not something we *do*, purpose is something we *are*. And *to be* is a lot more solid and lasting than *to do*. Jesus encouraged us to build our houses on solid foundations, and one of the most solid foundations we can build on is to know who we are before we try to figure out what we're supposed to do. If we believe our purpose centers in something we do, what happens if we can't do it anymore? We are way too vulnerable to feelings of inadequacy, depression, restlessness, and lostness when we rely on the external nature of purpose!

Laying Strong Foundations

My husband and I once built a new house. We checked on it nearly every day. What were we looking for? Initially, we wanted to make sure there were no cracks in the basement floor or walls. As the structure grew, we wanted to be certain the flooring and wall structure were stable and strong. We looked for sound electrical and plumbing connections so when we were using our home on an everyday basis, we wouldn't be caught with the unpleasant surprise of an electrical fire or burst pipe. Granted, all of this groundwork wasn't very glamorous or showy, but without it the decorating that we were going to do when we moved in would be just a veneer over problems that would eventually erupt.

This book is all about laying good foundations. There are three parts that will each build on the one that came before. When you are finished, you will feel solid from the very base of your being. You will have built a strong, personal purpose structure with strong groundwork, sturdy flooring, and well-supported walls and roof.

God's Two-Tiered Plan

God has given each of us two kinds of assignments. The first is a set of assignments that are universal. Everyone has been given these assignments. I call this the "Call for All." The second kind of purpose is very individual and specific. This is what I call "Divine Assignment."

In Part 1, we will look at the three basic calls on a Christian's life. This is the foundation from which we'll work as we each discover our particular and unique call. Looking at the three parts will be a lot like participating in a baseball game. When you are up to bat and hit the ball, you must run to and tag first base before you can go on and tag up on second base. Once you have covered first and second base, you can advance to third, tag up, and then head for home. The first three pieces we will look at will be the first three bases we all need to cover before we can truly get a handle on and authentically and satisfyingly live our own particular purpose.

Part 2 will enable you to focus on the particular purpose God has sent you to earth to live. This purpose will be a combination of one primary passion and one essential strength. The combination of these two elements is unique to you. I can guarantee your heart will beat faster and your eyes will sparkle as you get a laser-focused vision for why you are here on the planet. You will begin to realize who you are.

Part 3 is about *do*. It is the third part of the book because you can't authentically *do* anything truly satisfying until you know who you *are*. Don't skip to Part 3! That would be building on a faulty foundation. In this implementation section, we will explore how your Divine Assignment will give you more satisfaction in the roles you play, the gifts and skills you have to carry out your purpose in your work, and the challenges and situations you need to attend to every day as you live your Divine Assignment. In Part 3 you'll start to "write the vision, and make it plain" as God told Habakkuk (Habakkuk 2:2).

The Eternal Question—What's in It for Me?

How will your life improve by knowing and living your Divine Assignment? First and foremost, you will become a solid, strong, whole person. C.S. Lewis, in his classic *The Great Divorce*, describes a pathetic ghost who has ridden a bus out of hell to heaven, trying to make an impression on the creatures of heaven. She is garish and wispy. She believes she is beguiling and alluring when she is actually pitiful, frail, and grotesque. Those living in heaven are substantial, firm, and rock-solid not only in their physical matter but also in their spiritual essence. These creatures have made the choice for understanding God as the true ground of their lives. When the ghosts of hell decide to drop whatever pretense they had that separates them from God, they go through a "thickening treatment" that "consists in learning to want God for His own sake."[1] In the Lord's Prayer we pray, "Your will be done on earth as it is in heaven." Heaven's intent is that we go through the process of becoming more substantial, strong, and sane as we go through the "thickening process" of embracing the Call for All, as well as discovering our Divine Assignments. It's an improvement we can begin on earth.

Second, you will become a much better steward of your resources. This will be a relief to you, especially as you learn to say yes and no with certainty and grace when there are requests (or demands) for your energy and talents. You will spend your money and time more wisely as you home in on what's really important to you and where you feel your resources are best used. When you know what you believe and what you're good at, you can make better choices about what activities and causes to become involved in. You'll find yourself more and more satisfied with your everyday life because it's not cluttered with lots of things you're committed to that divert your passion and energy from things you really want to be centered on. My good friend Amy, who learned the power of saying yes and no with greater authenticity and confidence, introduced me to a wonderful quote by Annie Besant: "What I have not time to do is not my work." MaryAnn gives a compelling description of what this means in real life:

> The key thing that I have enjoyed in working through my Divine Assignment is that it *frees me* to focus on just one thing. It seems that I have been blessed (or perhaps cursed) with more good opportunities for work, fellowship, and family activities than I can possibly do and still come even close to enjoying them and be a decent person for my family to live with. If my assignment from God is to encourage home, then I can *give myself permission* to say no to the things that don't fit within that scope.
>
> As an example, for the past several years I have served on my church's Christian Education team. This year I was asked to become a deacon. I know

that I can't do two sets of nightly meetings at church. I also know that Christian Education at our church sorely needs dedicated people to help our children. But the other deacons at our church do many projects with the sole goal of encouraging hope within our church and the neighborhood community. In particular, one of the projects is to serve the children and teachers at School 54, for the free lunch program.

After much thought, that is where I have decided that my efforts should go—to help those children have hope.

MaryAnn is married, the mother of two little girls, an attorney, and deeply committed to her community. She's active and involved—she's a lot like you. We all need to know when to say yes and when to say no for the sake of our sanity, our best and most satisfying contribution, our greatest enjoyment, and the safety of those around us.

Dive into the Riches of Life with God

We live in a culture where we can drive up to the ATM to get instant cash. We can open cartons and cans to get instant food. So this book will offer you something that is, hopefully, a refreshing break from our culture. There is nothing instant about discovering your Divine Assignment. *It is a process.* While you will certainly encounter moments in this process in which you feel you make giant leaps forward, you will also realize that your entire lifetime is the timeline for discovering and implementing your Divine Assignment. The point is that you have to get started, and you have to have a set of tools to help you determine where you're going and how you're doing in the transformation. That's precisely why I applaud you for choosing this book. It will help you get started and includes a well-tested set of tools to stay on course. Most of all, it will point you to the partner you have who is constantly with and in you to make your transformation deep, exciting, and richly satisfying. I offer this book and this process to you "being confident of this, that he who began a good work in you will carry it on to completion until the day of Christ Jesus" (Philippians 1:6).

We are going to walk through this discovery process together. I realize I may be joining a group of you or working with you as an individual. But this process is something we're taking step-by-step, each step building on the one before. This is a highly dynamic process with much of the chapter content devoted to interactive questions. I strongly suggest you get a notebook or a journal of some kind to use as you interact with the "Discovering More About You" sections at the end of each chapter—a Divine Assignment log book, if you will. You might also want to cut out meaningful quotes and pictures from books and magazines that God may lead you to during the process. You may run across a piece of poetry, or design a piece yourself, that you want to include. Song lyrics or original drawings may emerge that need to go into this notebook or journal. You may find you are writing something of an autobiography as you go through this self-discovery progression. And please do yourself a loving favor: As you encounter questions in the chapters and the Discovering More About You sections, don't stop and ask yourself, "I wonder what she means by that?" It means whatever it needs to mean to you. There are no "right" answers. As your intention is growth and getting to know yourself and God better to more effectively minister to your world, you can't really mess up. Engaging in this process is a lot like what I tell my friends when we're making rubber-stamped cards—you can't make a mistake. The only mistake is putting this off and not diving into the riches of life with God, discovering his hopes and visions for you.

As you prepare to move into the grand adventure set out in this book, ask and answer four questions in your Divine Assignment notebook:

1. What are you seeking to learn in this self-discovery?
2. What has brought you to this place of wonder and discovery?
3. What is your greatest joy in life at this time?
4. What is your greatest challenge in life at this time?

Discovering your Divine Assignment is a process of understanding who you are and why you are on this earth. It takes some time, some intentional conversation (which involves talking and listening) with your Creator, ruthless honesty, and a keen understanding that you matter. Your character matters, your talents matter, your desires and passions matter, your very existence in this world matters. You are here for a reason that involves who you *are* first, then what you *do*.

From God's Perspective

God has hopes and visions for you. Before you were born, God had in his mind and in his heart all of the purposes he designed for your life. Purpose in God's heart is not only what you were meant to do; in fact, what you're meant to do is rather secondary to the hopes and visions God has always had for you. As you were being formed, God envisioned that you would know love—complete love. God pictured you finding joy in your community. God hoped you would discover the special gifts, talents, and interests he gave you so that you could feel great glee in using them to make a contribution for his sake in his world. All of that is to lead you to God's greatest hope and desire for you—that you and he be connected in a dynamic relationship of mutual love. That's what God wants for you. Everything else is to lead you to that place and to ensure that you want to stay there.

I wish you joy in the journey.

Part 1

Freedom for All

And what does the LORD require of you?
To act justly and to love mercy
and to walk humbly with your God.

MICAH 6:9

ONE

Unencumbered Enthusiasm!

❧

We are the wire, God is the current.
Our only power is to let the current pass through us.

CARLO CARRETTO

In the 1986 movie *Hoosiers*, Gene Hackman plays coach Norman Dale who comes to a tiny Indiana town at the invitation of a college friend. Hackman is a man with a checkered past looking to make a fresh start for himself as well as to bring out the best in the small group of young men who form the 1954 Hickory High School basketball team.

Hackman ruffles more than a few feathers as he insists that the boys focus on the fundamentals of the game, such as dribbling, passing, conditioning, defense, and teamwork. The boys (and the townspeople) have been focused on shooting, especially the shooting of one star player, Jimmy. After all, shooting the ball is the only way to make points. Yet day after day in practice, with Coach Dale at the helm, the boys work on the fundamentals.

Why should we tend to the fundamentals first? As Coach Dale proves, fundamentals help us keep our wits about us when we are faced with adversity. Fundamentals build a strong foundation that helps us stay disciplined and focused, laying the base for true (and sometimes hidden) talent to shine. Fundamentals help us keep our "head in the game" when outside forces seek to distract and derail us. In the end, the Hickory High School team accomplishes something no school of their size had done to that point and no school of their size has done since—win the state championship title in basketball.

When we tend to the basics, we develop something that biblical writers emphasized: a pure heart. The psalmists ask for pure hearts. Jesus urges us to develop a pure heart and gives us a very compelling reason to do so—the pure in heart shall see God (Matthew 5:8). If you want a clearer notion of your Divine Assignment, you need to see God.

The pure in heart shall see God. Only when we see God will we get a true notion of our Divine Assignment.

The Call for All

The fundamentals of God's call on our lives are simple but extraordinary. We are to receive and respond to God's love, love ourselves, and love others.

Jesus had a remarkable way of cutting to the heart of the matter. When he was asked what was most important to living a life that was pleasing to God, he said, quoting from Deuteronomy and Leviticus, "'Love the Lord your God with all your heart and with all your soul and with all your mind.'... And the second is like it: 'Love your neighbor as yourself'" (Matthew 22:37-39). Jesus wasn't telling us anything new, but he was boiling down pages and pages of written law into two succinct commandments that would keep us busy for the rest of our lives if we took them seriously.

We love the Lord our God when we have a true understanding of the Lord our God. Otherwise we can be indifferent to, afraid of, hostile toward, but not in love with God.

We grow to be in love with our God by receiving and responding to his love for us. This is the first assumption Jesus makes in these commandments. He assumes that to know God is to love God. To have a Divine Assignment means we have a Divine Assigner. And we need to know the truth of his nature before we can get a clear and authentic understanding of his assignment for us.

The second basic is to love ourselves. Loving ourselves is not the same as being obsessed with ourselves. We will unpack this concept in chapter 3. The three basic elements of loving ourselves are self-awareness, self-understanding, and self-acceptance.

The third basic is to love others. As with the other two basics, this call is extended to and expected of all. Loving others isn't something that some of us are called to do and some of us aren't. Although this may be a difficult call, it is foundational to our effectiveness in our distinct Divine Assignments. As we'll see when we get to the particular purpose each of us has been given, none of these distinct Assignments can be authentically enacted until we truly love and are concerned for others.

The Call for All

1. Love God
2. Love yourself
3. Love others

The Bottom Line on Basics

Richard N. Bolles, the author of the definitive book on career placement *What Color Is Your Parachute?* and a deeply devoted Christian, described each of these calls in *How to Find Your Mission in Life* as "one which you share with the rest of the human race, but it is no less your individual Mission for the fact that it is shared."[1] In other words, simply because all human beings have the call to receive and respond to God's love doesn't mean it's not intensely meant for each of us individually. Just because all are called to the basics to love ourselves and love others doesn't mean each of these calls won't be played out in distinct and unique ways in each of our lives. The "Call for All" is not a one size fits all. We are all meant to wear each of them.

The basics are lifelong. They will take us our whole lives to master, and even then we'll never get to the bottom of what it means to love as God asks us to love. So it's not like we cover them, get them all handled, and *then* get our Divine Assignment. Our Divine Assignment becomes clearer as the heart becomes more clear. And the heart becomes more clear as we follow the first and second great commandments: love God and love our neighbor as ourselves.

The absolute bottom line is receiving and responding to God's love, as we'll uncover in the next chapter.

Discovering More About You

From your point of view and experience, fill in the blank for each sentence.

1. God is _____.

2. I am _____.

3. Other people are _____.

4. To be happy, I need _____.

5. God meets me when _____.

6. The basics _____.

❧

Gracious God,

Right now I'm eager to get down to the particular purpose you have for me. Give me the patience and wisdom to see that in building a strong foundation, I will better be able to discern your unique Assignment for me when the time comes.

Help me to open myself to you so that I may more fully enter into the loving and dynamic relationship you desire with me. Help me open myself so that I can honestly get a better sense of all that I am and all I am capable of. Help me be more open to my community—to all the people around me—and to have a more genuine relationship of giving and receiving.

Be working in my heart even now so that I can better receive and respond to your mind-boggling love.

In Christ's name, amen.

Two

God's Greatest Vision for You

❧

*Live wholeheartedly, be surprised,
give thanks and praise—then you
will discover the fullness of your life.*

BROTHER DAVID STEINDL-RAST

Ever play the game "Two Truths and a Lie"? It's often used as an ice breaker for groups who are just getting to know each other. The object is to tell the others in the group three facts about yourself. Two of these facts should be the truth, and one of the facts should be a lie. The others in the group try to guess which one is the lie. Not only can you find out some interesting truths about a person, you can also find out what they think makes a good lie.

This chapter could be called "One Truth and Many Lies." There is one fundamental, basic, not-to-be-tampered-with truth in this universe. That truth is God loves you deeply, passionately, unconditionally, and eternally. No other truth can heal your restless psyche, your bruised ego, your shattered dreams, or your inappropriate opinions of yourself. It is the first truth we're called to believe before we can understand and live our Divine Assignments.

Why is it that the things that are the simplest are the hardest for us to believe? We are interesting creatures who tend to make things more difficult, convoluted, and inaccessible than they are. As Ezra Pound said, "Man is an over-complicated organism. If he is doomed to extinction he will die out for want of simplicity." Maybe it's the intensity of simple truth that makes us want to muddy the waters so we don't have to understand and be transformed. Whatever the reason, there isn't a more uncomplicated truth than we find in John's first epistle: "God is love" (1 John 4:16).

There you have it. Short and sweet. What is there to argue about? But all of us have a difficult time receiving and responding to God's love at one time or another. Some of us struggle with it every day. Why?

What Color Is Your Lemon?

We each have a set of glasses through which we see reality. Based on our genetics and our environment (what happened to us and around us as we were growing up), we have different colored lenses through which we see reality. And there is no more real reality than the love of God.

So if the love of God is like a lemon, and you are wearing a pair of glasses that are tinted blue with self-deprecation, depression, discontent, or just a general blah feeling about life, what color is the lemon?

If the love of God is like a lemon, and you are wearing a pair of glasses that are tinted red with anger, envy, entitlement, or ingratitude, what color is the lemon?

If the love of God is like a lemon, and you are wearing a pair of glasses that are tinted gray through ambition, busyness, self-sufficiency, or disinterest in God, what color is the lemon?

In all three cases, the lemon is yellow. The lemon is always yellow. But we may believe we see a green, orange, or murky gray lemon. But the lemon is really always yellow. And until we get a pair of glasses with clear lenses—in other words, a pure heart—we won't be able to see God in a perspective that truly sets the stage for us living our Divine Assignments.

What Keeps You from God?

The reasons we feel separated from God are as unique to each of us as we are from each other, but they do seem to fit into several general categories.

1. We're doing just fine, thanks. We get separated from God when things are going too well, and we get a little full of ourselves. We may forget to express thanksgiving for all of God's benefits.

2. We've gotten out of touch. With so many things going on in life, so many people to interact with, and so few moments to just be still, we seem to have lost our connection with God. For many, keeping a consistent Bible-reading time in their schedules makes a difference. Jody notes the difference in her connection to God in this way: "I sense that I have wandered from him when I am not in the Word on a daily basis. The living, breathing presence of the Holy Bible must be in my life each day to experience the awesome presence of God. When I am not in this mode, I feel stressed, less patient with my children, and tired."

3. We've done something disobedient that we know we shouldn't have done, and we feel we are out of God's plan. Sin is anything that separates us from God because it's a violation of the overarching codes of spiritual health that are given to each of us to help us stay on track. When a code is violated, we feel separated.

4. We find intimate relationships challenging. Perhaps as children we were ignored, abused, or otherwise found it difficult to make attachments to important people in our lives. Because God is the ultimate authority figure,

as well as the being with whom we can be most intimate, issues with intimacy or attachment may play a
big role in an inability to develop a close and loving
relationship with God.

5. We've gotten absorbed into our own world, our own
   problems, our own internal workings.

Remember: The first basic Call for All is to receive and
respond to the love of God.

Used but Not Loved

Have you ever been in a relationship where you eventually
felt like more of a utility to the other person than someone he
or she deeply and genuinely cared about? The problem with
so many people who are talking about the purpose God has
for each of us is that they are focused on being "used" by
God. The main emphasis is "How can God use me?" When we
are concentrating on being used by God, that's usually how we
end up feeling—used. We can feel like little puppets at the
disposal of a puppet master whose foremost concern is that
we perform well. Puppets are never partners with their
puppet masters, they are never partners who walk hand-in-
hand with their creators to bring transformation to themselves and to others.

When we first and always attend to the fact that God loves
us deeply, passionately, and eternally, we are much more likely
to have the healthy perspective we need regarding our place
in the world. This frees our hearts to more joyful and grateful
service. Jesus himself made this relationship distinct and clear
when he said, "I no longer call you servants, because a servant
does not know his master's business. Instead, I have called you
friends, for everything that I learned from my Father I have
made known to you" (John 15:15). We are not used as slaves
of God; we are *partners* with God, just as Jesus partnered with
God. We are indeed servants, but our servanthood is lived out
through an identity that we are friends of God serving others.

Our love affair with God involves two basic stance husband, a marriage-and-family therapist, is fond of te premarital couples that for the maximum health in their rela-tionship, they will have two postures with each other. The first stance is face-to-face. The time spent face-to-face in a love affair brings the lovers closer together as they get to know each other, care for each other, openly express affection for each other, and concentrate on nurturing and nourishing the relationship between the two of them. The second stance they will have, once the first has been satisfied, is facing out together. This position is one of service, of focusing on the community around them to meet needs and make contribu-tions, having been fortified and uplifted by the love between them. It's really a very similar dynamic with God.

Our outward service to others in the name of Jesus is most heartfelt and genuine and more sustainable over the long haul when we have had the face-to-face time with God that leaves little room for doubt that he loves us deeply, passion-ately, unconditionally, and eternally.

Concentrating on how we are "used" can actually make us a little egocentric and narcissistic as we're always wondering how we're doing or if others are noticing. Fixed on the love of God, we are free to stop wondering how we're doing or what others think. Being absorbed by God's enormous love for us gives us the "heart of wisdom" we need to make the most of our days.

The very first question of the Westminster Confession asks, "What is the chief end of man?" The very first answer of the Westminster Confession is "to glorify God, and to enjoy him forever." None of us can glorify God without truly knowing God. Once we have a clearer picture of who God is through spending time truly understanding how he feels about us, what his attributes are, and what his hopes and intentions are for the world and for us, we honestly can't help but glo-rify God. We can authentically enjoy God once we have a clear picture of his true nature. Any hesitation we have in either of these two aspects of our relationship with him—glorify or enjoy—is a great clue that we still don't have a pure heart, a clean window through which God can reveal his true self to us.

Essential Perspective

In his remarkable book *The Call*, Os Guiness ends each of the chapters this way: "Listen to Jesus of Nazareth; answer his call." When I was younger and read the book, although I thought the sentiment was nice, my response was often, "Yes, yes. I get it. I love Jesus dearly, but I have things I need to be doing. Now just tell me what to do." In my eagerness to make an impression on the world, I was glossing over the essential and basic truth that Jesus is at the very core of my being. I truly am a grape on the vine that withers and dies if it tries to do something apart from the source (see John 15:5-8). Christians, especially long-time Christians, need to be ever vigilant against becoming complacent about God's love and power and centrality in our lives.

To say we have a Divine Assignment indicates there is a Divine Assigner. The primary call we have in life is to get to know the Assigner. The foundational source of life—any kind of life with meaning—is to look to a relationship with God first. Searching for any kind of Divine Assignment while putting the Assigner on the back burner will leave us restless with emptiness and uncertainty.

How we get to know God depends on our temperament, on the resources and challenges of our backgrounds, and on our ability to seek God for ourselves with our whole hearts. Getting to know God takes critical thinking and critical feeling, testing the spirits, mulling things over, searching instead of swallowing hook, line, and sinker the doctrine or dogma of our past or our present.

If you feel unloved, unvalued, shamed by what others have led you to believe about God, or you feel you have to be defensive about your beliefs, you are not resting in the true love of God. God's love will never make you feel ashamed. God's love never requires that you defend it, only live it.

On God's Terms

Funny thing about us humans, we usually like things on our own terms. We feel safer when we can spell out exactly what we want. To a certain extent, this is a healthy expression of who we are, and it keeps us on good terms with other people. But we need to go to God on *his* terms.

What are God's terms? Historical American Christianity has done a disservice to some of us when it comes to what we think God's terms are. We have been given some rigid and/or outrageously depersonalized guidelines as to what God's terms are for entering into relationship with him. Understandably, some of us held off as long as we could in becoming close to God because the terms we were taught didn't really match what our God-given intuition told us about love.

Lewis Smedes, in his final book, *My God and I: A Spiritual Memoir,* brings God's expectations of us to startling clarity.

> But [God] met me again at a used book store. I was browsing there, picked up a thin volume called *The Rest of Faith,* and read it in the aisle between the stacks. The author, whoever he was, told me that if I wanted to come to terms with God, it had to be on his terms, the chief one being that I would have to give up my ridiculous notion that I would be accepted by God only if I had what it took to be [a particular] type. What I needed to do was let him accept me with no consideration of whether I was either acceptable or unacceptable. And then, when I had done that, to quit stewing about it and just rest in the fact that I was loved and accepted by God, no strings attached. Odd that it should have taken me so long to get the point.[1]

God's terms are "No strings attached." And it gets even better. Not only are there no strings attached, but God has powerful gifts to give you to prove that you can quit stewing about his acceptance of you and just rest in his love.

Freedom—I am amazed by how many people talk about the relief they feel when they realize they are free because of God's love. For some, freedom means they can express themselves as they never thought they could. Once people start reading the psalms and realizing the wide range of emotions that the psalmists cover, they realize they too can express incredible joy, unfathomable disappointment, mind-numbing despair, and sweet peace without reservation because God already knows their hearts and, furthermore, God can handle whatever they're feeling.

Others are set free from the captivity of the stranglehold of regret or shame. Still others realize they are no longer slaves to the opinions of the culture or people who had previously held great power over them. Freedom also comes from realizing there is more to eternity than what we see here, so we are free to think beyond the boundaries of grief over losing a loved one or past the despair when this life doesn't hold everything for us that we once thought it would.

Why are we free? Because God's love was made evident to us through the life of Jesus. Jesus told all who were around him, "Anyone who has seen me has seen the Father" (John 14:9). Jesus set people free by reassuring them of his place with God, then letting them know they were children of God as well.

> To the Jews who had believed him, Jesus said, "If you hold to my teaching, you are really my disciples. Then you will know the truth, and the truth will set you free." They answered him, "We are Abraham's descendants and have never been slaves of anyone. How can you say that we shall be set free?" Jesus replied, "I tell you the truth, everyone who sins is a slave to sin. Now a slave has no permanent place in

the family, but a son belongs to it forever. So if the Son sets you free, you will be free indeed" (John 8:31-36).

And why have we been set free? "It is for freedom that Christ has set us free. Stand firm, then, and do not let yourselves be burdened again by a yoke of slavery" (Galatians 5:1). Recognizing and receiving God's love means we embrace our freedom when sin tries to tie us down or when other negative influences try to weigh us down. Only you know where you are susceptible to slavery in your life. To let God love you is to recognize his hope and intention that you be free.

Full life—Jesus laid out his Divine Assignment succinctly when he said, "I have come that they [his sheep] may have life, and have it to the full" (John 10:10). To get a complete picture of what life to the full could look like, it's fun to see all the different definitions there are of "full."

Full is the opposite of empty. An empty life has holes from lost careers, from broken relationships, from having chased the wrong stuff for so long. We have empty lives when we have so much going on that we don't take time to nourish ourselves and our connection with God and those who are meaningful to us. We feel empty when we go through a transition that alters our understanding of our identity and leaves us shells of what we once felt ourselves to be.

Full is the opposite of hungry. When we're hungry, we look for something to satisfy us. A bit of hunger can be a good thing because it may keep us restless and continually searching for a way to make things better. But the full life Jesus talks about is one in which there aren't any gnawing hungers that hurt our hearts and souls without relief: "Blessed are those who hunger and thirst for righteousness, for they will be filled" (Matthew 5:6).

Fullness is the opposite of thinness. Our lives can just be plain scrawny. Our spirit of generosity or gratitude may be emaciated because we've lost our focus on God. Maybe the time we spend nourishing ourselves is lean due to lack of self-appreciation or everyday circumstances that crowd out the self-care we so desperately need to stay healthy.

Fullness is also the opposite of sketchy. Contrast a full-color oil masterpiece painting with the beginning sketches the artist did when he or she was first conceptualizing the work. The artist of your life—God—wants you to receive and respond to his love because he knows that when you do, your life will become rich with color and luster. Clarity will come into your life as you embrace more thoroughly who you are and whose you are.

Peace—"Peace I leave with you; my peace I give you....Do not let your hearts be troubled and do not be afraid" (John 14:27). Jesus spoke these words to his disciples at a crucial point in their relationship. He had been talking to them about his true identity and what would be happening in their near future. They were trying to make sense of all the radical spiritual truth Jesus was giving them, which challenged what they had always known. They were in spiritual transition. Have you ever felt that way? Have you ever been in a situation where what you have always known and seen is reframed by increased spiritual awareness and a call to a deeper relationship with God? Most of what troubles us is actually in that category. What troubles your heart? Is it a relationship? Is it a financial situation? Is it the past and the ghosts that keep emerging and reemerging? Meeting God on God's terms means expanding what you believe or expect to include a deeper awareness of God's workings and intentions in your life. This brings peace.

Hope—If we want to be loved on God's terms, we need to give ourselves the freedom to enjoy the hope that he offers. Paul says God is the "God of hope" (Romans 15:13). Hope in him brings peace and joy as we learn to trust him more deeply. God wants us to "overflow with hope by the power of the Holy Spirit" (Romans 15:13). To live in hope means to live with optimistic anticipation, to have a trusting faith that all we see is not all there is. God is always at work, at play, to bring meaning, health, and wholeness. We may have to endure waiting when things appear out of control or hopelessly discouraging. But it's only temporary:

> And we rejoice in the hope of the glory of God. Not only so, but we also rejoice in our sufferings, because we know that suffering produces perseverance; perseverance, character; and character, hope. And hope does not disappoint us, because God has poured out his love into our hearts by the Holy Spirit, whom he has given us (Romans 5:2-5).

Reconciliation—The bottom line of God's terms for the relationship he desires with us is reconciliation. This is the platform on which freedom, abundant life, peace, and hope rest. Reconciliation is more than just being pardoned for our wrongs. Reconciliation is God throwing his arms open wide and inviting us to be his friends. Reconciliation goes beyond wiping the slate clean. It tosses the entire slate in the trash, never to be used again to tally the lapses, blunders, and faults we have in our lives everyday.

> You see, God is either the God of perfect grace...or he is not God. Grace forgets. Period. He who is perfect love cannot hold grudges. If he does, then he isn't perfect love. And if he isn't perfect love, you might as well put this book down and go fishing, because both of us are chasing fairy tales.
>
> But I believe in his loving forgetfulness. And I believe he has a graciously terrible memory.[2]

Reconciliation may quite possibly be the hardest of God's terms to accept. When we believe in this kind of forgiveness, the kind based on God's forgetfulness, we can experience unlimited freedom in living an abundant life filled with peace and a sense of hope that does not disappoint because it's not grounded in only what we see, but also what we know. And through God's grace, we have to learn to forget as well.

Cherished by God

God is not complicated. Human beings sometimes like to make him complicated so we don't have to face his simple truths and fall in love with him as he already is with us. But Jesus gives a straightforward description in the Sermon on the Mount of those who will fully understand God's love and be more fully able to receive and respond to it: The pure in heart will see God (Matthew 5:8).

Purity in this respect doesn't mean perfection; otherwise, none of us would ever see God. Purity is not "we have to be perfect or God won't play with or accept us." Purity compares to a clean window—we can see better and be better seen. There is nothing between God and us that hinders communication or connection. Purity has to do with intent, with staying uncluttered, and with maintaining a singular focus. When we keep our intention toward seeking God, keeping clear of the many burdens we can so easily pick up along the way and remaining in a posture of welcoming God's grace, we will have pure hearts. We will see God. And in seeing God, we can't help but receive and respond to the love of God.

Do you honestly know in your heart of hearts that you are cherished by God? Do you know that you can truly be completely centered and dependent on God? On an everyday basis do you enjoy and/or glorify God? Do you understand and embrace that God likes you as much as he loves you?

Why do we need to receive and respond to God's great love for us? Because it's the only hope we have of being the kind of person who can do anything to truly make the world a better place. "We love because he first loved us" (1 John

4:19). We need to receive and respond to God's great love for us because it's the only antidote to fear, and it's fear that keeps us from anything good, both in who we are and what we do.

Discovering More About You

1. Take a deep breath and, as you exhale, say to yourself, "God loves me deeply." Repeat the breathing and say to yourself, "God loves me passionately." Repeat one more time and say, "God loves me eternally." Write in your Divine Assignment book what it means to you that God loves you deeply, passionately, and eternally. What understanding is evoked by each word?

2. Is it difficult for you to fully receive God's love? Let past experiences and teachings come to light. What colored glasses are you wearing that distort the essential and simple truth that God loves you? Ask God what he truly thinks of those blocks and what he would like you to believe differently.

3. What's the difference between being used in a relationship and being a partner with someone else?

4. How is your face-to-face relationship with God at this point? How is your "facing out together" relationship? What needs to change in your life to facilitate both of those stances with God?

5. How have you been trying to meet God on your terms? What do you think of God's terms as described by Lewis Smedes?

6. What have you been a slave to in your life? What does freedom mean to you?

7. I feel empty when…
   My deepest hunger is…
   The scrawny part of my life…
   God's direction seems thin…
   Full life means…

8. How has God not only forgiven you but completely forgotten whatever you have done or not done? How does this kind of forgiveness impact your daily life?

9. Ask God what he wants you personally to know about this verse: "We love because he first loved us." Write his response.

❦

Dear God,

The most foundational truth of my being is your uncompromising love for me. Help me accept it on your terms—and your terms alone.

Show me how to have a pure heart—a heart that burrows into and stays immersed in your love for me. Give me a heart that is strong and tender. Give me a heart that is open and responsive to your love.

Increase my comprehension of who you are and who I am to your heart. I want to move into a deeper and fuller realization of how you want me to feel about myself and how you want me to treat others.

Thank you for your remarkable, deep, passionate, and eternal love.

In Christ's name, amen.

THREE

Am I Really Allowed to Do That?

❧

If you have some respect for people as they are,
you can be more effective in helping them
to become better than they are.

JOHN W. GARDNER

Isn't it funny how we can read the Bible for years assuming it says something, then read the same passage one day and something jumps out at us like never before? God is the God of surprises! That's one reason reading Scripture is so interesting. Same page, same verse, new revelation.

This is exactly what happened to me one Saturday afternoon as I was presenting at a women's retreat on this passage: "Love the Lord your God with all your heart and with all your soul and with all your mind and with all your strength....Love your neighbor as yourself" (Mark 12:30-31). Now, as a child, I was practically fed the "love God, love neighbor" part for breakfast every day, but what jumped out at me in the very act of reading the verse for the women was the basic assumption Jesus had that I had always missed. Jesus assumed that I would love myself. And that's the second basic Call for All—that we love ourselves.

It's All About Me

There is a bumper sticker slogan that just cracks me up. T-shirts and advertising campaigns are using it, too: "It's all about me." At first blush, I smile for all the poor folks who believe this to be true. At second glance, I smile more deeply for all the misguided people who don't believe it's true. Before you take me out to tar and feather me, let me explain why I think both ideas are true.

Some really well-intentioned Christians will vehemently decry a bumper sticker like that having been conditioned to respond with shame and blame to any sentence that has the word "me" in it. But as a Christian, it is first and foremost all about you! It's all about God loving *you,* redeeming *you,* calling *you* worthy. That's where the whole story starts between you and God. Humanly speaking, we will never truly be able to function with peace, dignity, zeal, or intentionality if we aren't first convinced that God's love is all about *us* first.

Now the paradox, of course, is that once we understand that God is crazy about us, then we can live lives *not* centered on us. When we have the peace that passes understanding, the peace that comes from being assured of our place in God's heart, we can embrace the truth that it isn't all about me, my accomplishments, my reputation, my worldly goods, and my comfort. We don't have to give in to the desire to be indulged, have the final word in all conversations, and be pampered to the exclusion of the needs, feelings, and lives of others.

Frankly, most of the time we're somewhere in the middle anyway, aren't we?

Uncomfortable with "Me"

We like ourselves; we don't like ourselves. That's why it's so hard to claim it's all about me. We know we are good and beloved. We know we are separated from God and not so good. How do we make it all work? The apostle Paul has such a wonderful handle on this in Romans 7:21–8:2:

So I find this law at work: When I want to do good,
evil is right there with me. For in my inner being I
delight in God's law; but I see another law at work
in the members of my body, waging war against the
law of my mind and making me a prisoner of the
law of sin at work within my members. What a
wretched man I am! Who will rescue me from this
body of death? Thanks be to God—through Jesus
Christ our Lord!...Therefore, there is now no condemnation for those who are in Christ Jesus,
because through Christ Jesus the law of the Spirit
of life set me free from the law of sin and death.

Paul says there's a me that's great, and there's a me that
isn't. There's a devil on one shoulder and an angel on the
other. The devil is constantly trying to convince me that I am
separated from God, that God doesn't care about me. When
I have divorced myself from the truth that, in God's eyes, his
love for me *is* all about me, I can give in to whatever destruc-
tive impulses I might have toward myself and toward others.

Once the angel or, more accurately, the Holy Spirit, convinces me that it is all about me when it comes to God's love
for me, then I am released to lay my obsession with myself
aside to focus on the lives of others and what God wants to see
happen in his world.

The Root of Self-Love

Many good-hearted people have a difficult time with the
concept of self-love. Confusing it with self-indulgence or self-
absorption, these folks won't acknowledge that they need to
be in a loving relationship with themselves. In its healthiest
form, self-love is recognizing our strengths and weaknesses
and making peace with them. My friend Sara defines it this
way: "Accepting myself just like I am...the way God has created me to be...just the way he planned because it's what he
needs to accomplish his plan. Not trying to be like someone

else whose gifts/ministry I admire; rather, accepting my gifts/ministry as what God needs from me to 'complete the body.'" How do we come to this kind of wholesome self-love?

Where does Jesus want us to "remain" or linger or hang out? He says, "Remain in my love" (John 15:9). God wants us to stay put in his love. Get there and stay there. And believe me, we can't hang out for any period of time in God's love without discovering that the way God feels about us can be trusted, and we can indeed love ourselves. If God loves us, who are we to disagree? Do we think we know more or better about ourselves than God does? God's estimation of us needs to be the standard for how we feel about our redeemed selves.

There are three indispensable elements to loving ourselves as God wants us to that set the stage for a richer, deeper understanding of our particular Divine Assignments. To get a clear picture of ourselves and the love we need to have for ourselves before we can experience deep joy in contributing to others, we need self-awareness, self-understanding, and self-acceptance.

Self-Awareness

Psychologists tell us that the first time we really start to be self-aware is when we're around two years old. It is self-awareness that prompts us to say no, to the dismay of people around us, who then taught us to think like they do so we would stay safe and not cause them embarrassment, hardship, or inconvenience. We were taught to ignore our own feelings. As a result, many of us don't have a well-defined sense of self-awareness. Early conditioning suggested that we deny what we need or want, that we disallow the personal boundaries we wanted to set for ourselves. We rejected what our inner selves told us. The conflict between what our newly forming selves communicated with us and what our authority figures dictated for us was so strong that we took the road of least resistance. We embraced the best option we had for outer comfort and acceptance—self-extinction.

Often the first step in moving from self-extinction to healthy self-awareness is listening to the little gnawing feeling that something in your life just isn't quite right. We have those feelings when we are out of alignment with who we were created to be, often signaling that we are trying to be something we're not, trying too hard to get someone else's approval, ignoring what we really feel is the right response to a situation, or not standing up for what we know to be the right way to treat others.

For example, a young child my be shamed at the dinner table for not liking a certain kind of food and voicing that opinion. Adults see this as especially offensive when they are eating at someone else's home. The child may be forced to eat the food, negating his stated preference. The child may be sent away from the table, indicating that if you don't do things the way we want you to, you can't be part of this community. The child may be teased and mocked for not eating what he clearly doesn't like. Over time, the child learns not to trust his or her own preferences because bad things happen when he speaks his opinions or likes and dislikes.

Or a child may be abused by someone who is in authority to him. The authority figure makes the child believe the abuse is the child's fault, that the child deserves it, or may lead the child to believe that it's normal for abuse to occur. Children know that it's not normal. They know that it hurts and it's wrong. But to stay in their family, to somehow manage the anxiety, anger, humiliation they feel, they learn to extinguish the little voice inside screaming that something is wrong. Over time, they practice self-extinction.

To move from self-extinction to healthy self-awareness, a person needs to come to an awareness of what is healthy, what promotes personal dignity, what brings a deep sense of peace, and what allows them to bring their unique opinions and contributions to the community.

True self-awareness restores personal boundaries, reaffirms personal preferences, and reestablishes the sense of healthy self we all need to preserve and protect the individual identity God gave us to make our unique contribution to the world. Self-awareness does not set us up in opposition to other people; it simply helps us understand how we are different from other people. Catherine insightfully commented, "There are things only I can do. Self-love means that for me to do the things only I can do, I have to love myself enough to take care of myself, to make time for myself, and to be myself."

Healthy self-awareness is central to authentically loving ourselves as God loves us. It helps us rejoice in what is good, change what isn't so great, and receive God's grace for what we haven't dealt with and what we can't change.

Self-Understanding

As a community college psychology teacher, one of my favorite assignments for my students is for them to articulate their own particular personalities. I do this to remind them that each of us is unique. No two of us are alike. We each have our own personality "print," just like we have distinctive fingerprints.

So how do we get to a place of self-understanding? By evaluating who we are and learning about us. Why don't you make an assessment of your personality traits? A trait is an attribute you have that reflects your attitudes, preferences, and styles of interaction. Each trait reflects a continuum, or a line with two extreme opposites at either end. We usually find ourselves somewhere in the middle of the two extremes, often leaning toward one or the other. Where do you find yourself on the continuum of these 10 personality traits?

1. *Reserved/Warm*—Are you a person who smiles a lot at others, welcoming them into your life, or are you more likely to keep people a bit at arm's length? A reserved person is slower to open up to others and prefers to keep things more private. A warm person is more outgoing and engaging to others on a regular basis.

2. *Avoids Conflict/Dominant*—Do you want to keep peace and try to be more of a compliant peacemaker in your relationships and in an assortment of situations? Or do you feel comfortable challenging people on a regular basis? One who avoids conflict will keep a low profile when he senses trouble may be brewing. The person who has a more dominant personality doesn't mind shaking things up with others.

3. *Serious/Lively*—If you have a serious personality, you are probably more likely to be described as stoic, stern, or unyielding. Liveliness, on the other hand, makes a person seem more approachable, fun-loving, and energetic. Are you more attracted to a quiet evening reading or having a deep conversation with a few people? Or are you more attracted to a fun-filled evening at a sporting event or in a group that's laughing and playing together?

4. *Trusting/Suspicious*—If you have a more trusting personality, you are more likely to be comfortable in believing people, making yourself vulnerable, and having faith that people will basically tend to try to do what's right and healthy. A more suspicious personality is cautious about opening up to people, has a worldview that people often have ulterior motives for their relationships and behavior, and that you have to keep on eye on people and situations so they stay in line.

5. *Practical/Imaginative*—When you see an oven mitt, do you say to yourself, "Now that's a fine oven mitt. Its purpose is to protect my hand when I take hot things out of the oven?" Or do you look at the oven mitt and see four additional ways in which it can be used? If you are more practical in your personality, you take relationships at face value and enjoy things for their intended purpose. If you have a more imaginative personality, you see the possibilities in an object or relationship that aren't apparent to everyone else. You are more creative. You think outside the box.

6. *Forthright/Private*—Do you tend to "tell it like it is" to anyone at any time? Or are you more likely to keep things under wraps? A forthright person steps up to the mike about any subject, speaking his mind, leaving no doubt in others as to how he feels about things. A private person believes there are proper topics for proper times with proper people. Others sometimes wonder where the private person stands on a topic or what he is thinking in a situation.

7. *Self-Assured/Apprehensive*—The self-assured personality usually doesn't need the approval of others to feel good about life. He believes in his ability to make good decisions. Self-assured people are confident that whatever others do in life, they will be able to respond in a healthy, self-affirming way. A more apprehensive personality tends to be unsure about their own abilities to either make things happen or make good decisions. Apprehensive people look to others for confirmation of their choices, affirmation of their ideas, and believe others hold the key to how they are going to feel about themselves.

8. *Traditional/Open to Change*—On one end of this continuum is the person whose favorite phrase is "We've always done it this way." For a more traditional personality, Thanksgiving just isn't Thanksgiving without the turkey, green-bean casserole, and pumpkin pie. The traditional person finds comfort in being able to count on people, relationships, and events to be the way they have been time after time. A person who is open to change is ready to have roast beef, steamed asparagus, and banana splits for Thanksgiving. They are not upset if people, relationships, and events are different than they were in the past. Open-to-change personalities find excitement in diversity and newness.

9. *Group-Oriented/Self-Reliant*—The group-oriented person draws on the coordinated talents of many people to get a job done. The self-reliant personality is more individualistic and

would rather take full responsibility for getting something done rather than depend on group process.

10. *Tolerates Disorder/Perfectionistic*—Would you be more comfortable in a family room that is "lived in" or one that has "a place for everything and everything in its place"? If you are a person who tolerates disorder, you don't mind if the counters and the calendar are cluttered. Your comfort in life is not based on knowing where everything and everyone are all the time. In fact, if things are too put together, you get a little nervous and feel stilted and uncomfortable. If you have a more perfectionistic personality, you will want your home, your family, and your schedule to be organized and orderly. Your idea of discomfort is to walk into a house that is cluttered, look at your calendar to find you have double scheduled, and not have people look and do as you expect.

That's a whole bunch of characteristics to reflect on. What did you notice about yourself? Did you see any patterns? Do you see how these traits affect your worldview?

We are each a remarkably unique amalgam of character traits. The more we understand ourselves, the better decisions we make about our relationships, our jobs, our involvements, and our responses to life.

Knowing why we are the way we are is the second highly potent factor in self-understanding, primarily because it helps us discern if we want to continue in a trait that has puzzled us or made us feel uncomfortable.

For example, if you have always been a person who tends to tolerate disorder, but you don't really like that about yourself, understanding where that trait came from can help you decide if you want to keep that trait or not. Perhaps you lived in a home where disorder was tolerated and any attempts you made to be more orderly were met with amusement at best, name-calling and scorn at worst. You may have decided it was easier to tolerate the disorder than to feel weird in your family, so you submerged your more perfectionist tendencies to keep the peace. But now you're grown and can make your own decisions about your God-given traits and tendencies. With the self-understanding that comes from knowing why you are the way you are, you can be more free to be completely who you were originally created to be.

How do you know when you are being who you were originally created to be? You will experience all of the benefits Christ talked about as he described people who were in line with what God hopes for each of us. You will have a sense of freedom that comes from not worrying about what other people think of you. You will be at peace even if you have to make decisions that aren't popular or highly regarded by the culture. You will have a sense of deep joy when you are engaged in activities that use your greatest gifts and most enjoyed talents. Freedom. Peace. Joy. Each is a sign that you are becoming the authentic you God created for his enjoyment and glory.

There are many more tools you can use to enhance your increase in self-understanding. The "Resources for Personality Assessment" in the back of this book will give you further options.

Self-Acceptance

Perhaps the hardest but most vital element in the process of loving ourselves as God loves us is self-acceptance. This concept gets all tangled up with the idea that if I accept myself, I may think I'm perfect, and there will be no place for God's grace and mercy in my life. But real self-acceptance is where self-awareness and self-understanding meet with a gentle welcoming of self and all that it was created to be. Gerald expressed this beautifully. "Self-love means being willing to love myself the way Jesus loves me, accepting my shortcomings, being gracious about any gift, and not allowing either to diminish the work he has called me to do." True self-acceptance knows I will always need God because he is the cornerstone of my existence. In being my most authentic self, I am completely reliant on God.

When we truly accept ourselves, we have a clear picture of what we're good at and what we aren't—and we don't sweat the latter. We may, for the fun of it, try something new from time to time, but we know we won't be an accomplished expert at everything. We may be placed in a mission that stretches us and causes us to move out of our comfort zone, but we always know that in the event of being called to do something that we have never done before, we are being called by the one who is more than willing and able to be our partner.

The most refreshing people I know are the ones who can say, "You know, I'm not really very good at what you just asked me to do. But I am really good in this other arena. Maybe I could help out in that way." Instead of trying to be all things to all people, instead of knowing that they really aren't equipped for everything and fearing others will find out, self-accepting people will be delighted by what they're good at and at peace with what they're not.

The bottom line on self-acceptance is this: I know who I am and who I'm not, and I'm comfortable with the fact that my Creator made me the way I am. God loves me and accepts me the way I am, why shouldn't I?

Crossing the Line

I had Elijah syndrome. Elijah was an Old Testament prophet who had a colorful, exciting, and sometimes dangerous career. The era of Old Testament history that he served was ruled by King Ahab and Queen Jezebel. They were infamous for their disrespect of and disdain for God, God's prophets, and the people of God. Elijah was called to bring God's reality to them and to all the people of the day. No small task.

A decisive and dramatic showdown between Elijah, the prophet of God, and the priests of Baal, the mouthpieces for

Ahab and Jezebel, tipped the scales in favor of Jehovah, Elijah's God. Elijah was so pumped up by the experience that, under the power of the Lord, he outran a king in his chariot to a neighboring city. Elijah was obviously very successful in this adventure.

What happened next is very interesting. Elijah, getting wind of Jezebel's all-points bulletin for his arrest and murder, fled the scene and ended up by the brooks of Cherith, living in a cave. After experiencing such striking emotions, so wide in their spectrum, Elijah collapsed in an exhausted state. He looked for God in the situation, hoping to be comforted and renewed. Given the dramatic nature of his recent experience, he expected more theatrics and stunning deliverance. It didn't come. But what did come was a still, small voice that told him to rest, to eat, to drink, and to sit tight while he was refreshed and protected.

I felt like Elijah after a nearly two-week trip that took me to two countries, three states, and six cities. I was on the road to talk about my first book with Harvest House Publishers, *Mom Overboard*. It was a wonderful trip. I met exciting and fascinating people, got a chance to talk to mothers all over the United States and Canada, ate wonderful meals that I didn't have to prepare myself, and even had a few quiet moments to think about upcoming projects. My itinerary had been well laid out by the Harvest House media staff, and I never missed a flight or arrived late to an appointment.

It wasn't until I got home that my enemies came after me. When I read through the psalms, sometimes I'm impressed that the enemies spoken of are as much internal as external. I seem to have formidable internal enemies. First of all, I was just plain physically tired. The enemy "Superwoman" reared its head against me, telling me I should just get over it. Was I a wimp or what? Couldn't I absorb a little physical exertion without getting exhausted?

Then the enemy "How did I do?" pitched the tent of self-doubt in my heart. I was afraid to look at the videotapes I had received from various producers. What if I had said stupid things? What if my hair looked remarkably dumb that day? What if all I had talked about didn't actually make a difference for people? What if Harvest House had wasted its money sending me out?

On the heels of that enemy came the "You should get a real job" adversary. I seem to always be vulnerable to the little imp who sits on my shoulder mocking me for being an entrepreneur and not contributing a steady income to the family. Sometimes my kids don't go places and do things other kids go and do because of my sporadic income. Sometimes I feel like my husband carries an inequitably heavy load as the regular paycheck earner. So for the sake of money, I'm often prey to second-guessing my real call, what I feel I'm really to be about in life. "Maybe I should just go to work at the local bookstore and be done with the self-doubt," I tell myself.

The last little critic that showed up was the "just get busy" critic. Just dust yourself off, stop being such a baby, do something productive—anything—and snap out of it!

I felt like Elijah. I was puzzled over the awe of having just had a wonderful experience yet feeling so spent and wondering about God's wisdom for having put me where I was. I was pretty self-obsessed. Then reality came. I learned that self-obsession is not the same as self-love. I was not loving to myself in the least. I was not caring for myself in a way that was going to help me regain my strength. I certainly wasn't open to and receiving God's love for me, although I really wanted to be. I was ruminating on self, wondering what kind of impression self was making. I was abusing self for not measuring up to whatever unrealistic and unhealthy standards I had taken on from childhood or the culture. Preoccupied with how my message was playing to all of the audiences I had addressed, I was measuring my effectiveness in book sales. I wasn't satisfied knowing that there would be some who disagreed with my message or couldn't find a way to implement it in their own lives. I was worried that I would be a failure and my family would be disappointed in and ashamed of me for not making a better impression or bringing in more income.

Some things just take time (and a little sleep) to work themselves out. As I look back on that time, I can now recognize that God was saying "Rest," and I just kept asking, "God what do you want me to *do?*" The Holy Spirit would smile and answer, "Rest." I would say, "Yes, I understand that, but what do you want me to *do?*" Truly resting doesn't come easily to most of us.

God wanted me to lighten up, to love myself as he loves me, and to remember that my only hope for sanity and effectiveness in this life is to play to the audience of one—him. God's opinion is the only one that matters, and his pleasure isn't necessarily measured in book sales, income generated, or pats on the back from others.

The truth is, until I truly love myself as God loves me, I'm doomed to be self-centered, self-indulgent, self-absorbed. It's our natural human response to feeling holes in our hearts, our souls, our psyches. When we feel empty we do all kinds of crazy things, hold all kinds of skewed attitudes, harbor inane feelings about ourselves and others. Loving myself as God loves me gives me the freedom I need to take my attention off myself, off healing my own wounds, off tooting my own little horn. Loving myself means to become unconscious of myself because "my needs" are now met.

Where do we go when we need a refresher course on love? Most of us turn to the very famous passage Paul wrote to the Corinthian church when they were struggling with what it means to be truly loving. He gives highly practical advice written in everyday terms:

> Love is patient, love is kind. It does not envy, it does not boast, it is not proud. It is not rude, it is not self-seeking, it is not easily angered, it keeps no record of wrongs. Love does not delight in evil but rejoices with the truth. It always protects, always

> trusts, always hopes, always perseveres. Love never
> fails (1 Corinthians 13:4-8).

While we may have a tendency to skim the contents because they have become so familiar, we would do ourselves a big favor to dig more deeply into what each aspect means, especially as we apply it to loving ourselves.

Love Is Patient

To be patient with myself means I don't fly off the handle with myself when I can't learn something quickly or when I let myself down for the hundredth time. It means I give myself the grace to fail, to try again, to take things slowly if needed.

If "patience is the companion of wisdom" as Augustine suggested, then patience goes hand in hand with the beautiful description of wisdom James gives in his New Testament letter: "But the wisdom that comes from heaven is first of all pure; then peace-loving, considerate, submissive, full of mercy and good fruit, impartial and sincere" (James 3:17). This kind of patient wisdom means I am peaceable with myself. I seek to keep things balanced and on an even keel. I am considerate of my feelings and my foibles. I don't get into the internal struggle of having to defend myself to myself if I have failed.

Remember the oyster and the grain of sand? The oyster recognizes that there is an irritation, something to be dealt with. But the oyster also uses its resources and a whole lot of patience to produce the pearl.

Love Does Not Boast or Is Proud

We all are made up of many parts, some that bring us satisfaction and happiness, some that bring us shame and regret. The apostle Paul seemed genuinely befuddled by the warring personalities that had residence in his one person. While we don't cling to the parts of us that embarrass us or cause us to stumble, we won't get rid of them by ridiculing them and belittling them.

They will only become healthy when they are coaxed to the surface and offered to God for wholeness and healing.

Paul knows that the sense of boasting or pride of which he speaks in 1 Corinthians cannot live in the same space as love because this attitude is actually fostered by a lack of true self-confidence or self-worth. When we see people boasting or bragging, we usually come away from them with a sense that they really don't genuinely feel good about themselves or they wouldn't need to make such a big deal out of themselves to impress others.

To love ourselves means we don't have to pump ourselves up with lots of blustery talk and grandiose notions of who we are. When we truly love ourselves, we don't have to "talk big" to make ourselves feel worthwhile. We know we're worthwhile because of who we are in God's world and in God's heart.

Now, of course, that's not to say that once in a while we don't need a pep talk. We certainly do. When we've been hurt by someone else, when we make a mistake, when we're having a bad day for any reason, we need to talk nicely to ourselves, reminding ourselves of all the good in our lives. By counting ourselves when we count our blessings, we give God a hand for doing a good job with us, just as he did with the rest of creation. But boastfulness or pride can't recognize the hand of God in the universe or in our own inner world.

Love Is Not Rude

The opposites of rude are courtesy and respect. Have you ever considered being courteous to yourself? Do you ever say things to yourself that you wouldn't think about saying to others? How often do you just blurt out "You're fat" or "You're way too thin" or "You are so stupid" or "You really blew it this time"? We talk so rudely to ourselves sometimes. We are disrespectful of the creation God called "good."

To be courteous to ourselves means we use civility in the way we treat ourselves and in the way we talk to ourselves. We

we are out of partnership with God, we can way too easily focus on the handicaps and not on the gifts. When we embrace who we are and who God is, we won't get confused about our shortcomings and our good qualities. To know the truth about ourselves means we have a healthy perspective on both, wearing the lenses God uses when he looks at us.

Love Hopes and Perseveres

When we apply hope and perseverance to ourselves, we're saying we believe that we can get better, that we should never give up on ourselves, that we keep pushing toward what we know is good about us in spite of evidence to the contrary.

Have you ever disappointed yourself? Disappointment in ourselves comes in many forms. We may feel ashamed that we blew the diet yet another day. We may be distressed because we didn't get all the work done this week that we wanted to get done. We may feel we have experienced a spiritual setback when we gave in to that pesky temptation one more time. We may feel the frustration of losing our tempers with those who are nearest to us and may be the most hurt. Disappointment can manifest itself as regret, displeasure, or a letdown feeling with ourselves.

We love ourselves in a First Corinthian's way when we embrace a thought for ourselves that Dr. Martin Luther King Jr. meant for a movement: "We must accept finite disappointment, but we must never lose infinite hope."[1] Giving yourself First Corinthian's love embodies the ability to understand that any disappointment we may have in ourselves is temporary. We can have infinite hope in ourselves because that's the way God sees us. Infinite hope gives us the eraser we need to get the blackboard clean again. Infinite hope—the kind of hope Jesus constantly offered to those around him while he was on earth, and the kind of hope his Holy Spirit whispers into our lives when our heads are hung and our cheeks streaked with tears—is the kind of hope we can give ourselves as part of the self-love process. We hope in ourselves and persevere in our good opinions about ourselves because God sees us that way. Who are we to argue with God?

When the outlook looks bleak and you don't feel like you're making much progress to anything good, just remember: "By perseverance the snail reached the Ark."[2]

The Truth About Integrity

To authentically love yourself, you need to live with integrity. Often when we think of integrity, we think of perfection, flawlessness, being above reproach. When we say someone lacks integrity, we mean they've done something dishonest, underhanded, perhaps immoral, and certainly unethical. This definition of integrity accounts for only one half of the authentic human experience—the limitations.

Integrity, at its root, has a radically different meaning. The Latin root means "whole" or "entire."

Parker Palmer, in his wonderful book *Let Your Life Speak,* suggests that living with integrity means we continually embrace the entirety of our humanity: "Each of us arrives here with a nature, which means both limits and potentials."[3] We accept ourselves in our wholeness, our entirety. Integrity doesn't mean we don't have imperfections or limitations. Integrity means we know what they are, and we are honest about them with ourselves and with God. The apostle John knew we would need to live in this complete and honest understanding if we were to be people of integrity: "If we claim to be without sin, we deceive ourselves and the truth is not in us" (1 John 1:8). This isn't meant to be a big red "A" like Hester has to wear in *The Scarlet Letter.* It's just a fact we need to accept and work with as we live our lives in partnership with God. Integrity means being aware of who we are, who God is, what God thinks about us, and receiving the provisions God has graciously made for our renewed and ever-renewing relationship with him.

Living with integrity allows us to dispel fear, self-abuse, and self-absorption. These distractions undermine the strong foundation Jesus encourages us to build for ourselves in the implication that we love ourselves when he cheers us on to love our neighbor as ourselves.

Integrity shares a root with a sibling word—"integral." Integral means lacking nothing essential. When we *receive and respond to God's love* and *choose to love ourselves as God loves us,* we have everything we need. Living with these essentials gives us the foundation to be and to do all that God hopes and envisions for us. With these two calls embraced and answered every day, the foundation is laid for the third part of the Call for All—loving others.

Discovering More About You

1. How do you react to the slogan "It's all about me"? If you were to make up a unique bumper sticker to express who it's all about, what would it say?

2. How can "knowing God's love *is* all about you" release you from being self-obsessed?

3. What is the root of self-love? Where are you denying God's great love for you simply because you won't believe that you can love yourself? What does it mean to you to "remain" in God's love?

4. What does self-awareness mean to you? On a scale of one to ten, with ten being very self-aware, how would you rate yourself in this area of self-love?

5. The second step in healthy self-love is self-understanding. This chapter gives you 10 different pairs of words to describe personality traits. For each pair of words:

   a. Identify where you are right now. Remember these are all on a continuum, so your description might indicate you are somewhere in the middle of the two identifying words.

   b. Give an example that illustrates why you think that about yourself.

   c. Identify where you would like to be if it's different from where you are.

   d. If you want to change where you are, identify the root of why you might be the way you currently are to see where you may need to change your thoughts, beliefs, expectations, or behavior.

6. The final step in self-love is self-acceptance. How does knowing that you are in a dependent relationship with God help you relax into self-acceptance? What parts of you don't you really want to accept but would be more at peace if you did? What parts of you do you accept with joyous gratitude?

7. What does it mean to be patient and kind with yourself? Where are you in need of these two expressions of love?

8. What does it mean to keep no record of wrongs for yourself? Where do you need to wipe the slate clean, knowing it's already been taken care of with God? Clear your account every day.

9. In embracing the "whole" of who you are, what limitations do you need to accept? What possibilities do you need to claim and keep in focus?

*L*oving God,

Thank you that you do indeed call me to love myself simply because I am your creation. Forgive me for the times I disrespect your creation by disregarding the wonder of me. Forgive me for the times I separate myself from the possibility of remaining in your love when I am self-obsessed or self-absorbed.

Lord, forgive me for the times I have bought into any input that wants to make me believe I am unworthy, not good enough, or unlovable. Clear away, by your Holy Spirit, the ghosts of the past or present that keep my view clouded from the truth you're constantly trying to get through to me.

God, there are going to be times in this part of my transformation when I will struggle with my true limitations and my authentic potential. Help me keep a clear vision of how you feel about me, for that's where the healthiest self-love comes from. Thank you that in you I can rest and rejoice in who I am.

In Christ's name, amen.

FOUR

Playground Rules for Life

❧

We live so close together.
So, our prime purpose in this life is to help others.
And if we can't help them, at least don't hurt them.

DALAI LAMA

When I was in kindergarten, my teacher gave my mother a report on my progress. Since five-year-olds rarely get academic grades, my teacher's assessment of my character was particularly noteworthy—it was all we had to go by at the time. My kindergarten teacher said to my mother, "She's a nice little girl, but she certainly is bossy." In other words, I didn't exactly play well with others!

The Worldwide Playground

The kingdom of God is like a playground. We're all in this big, worldwide community sharing equipment, choosing sides for games, running, resting, and learning how to get along with all the others on the playground.

The first basic Call for All is to love God. The second is to love ourselves. And the third basic is to play well with others. But we don't have to wait for a special call from God to know that we are to be nice, act graciously, and try to be helpful wherever we can. That's basic human decency to treat others with respect and care as we move through the day in the amazing rush of life. Richard Bolles calls this "The Spectacle Which Makes the Angels Laugh" and explains it this way:

> So many times you will see people wringing their hands, and saying, *"I want to know what my mission in life is"* all the while they are cutting people off on the highways, refusing to give time to people, punishing their mate for having hurt their feelings, and lying about what they did. And it will seem to you that the angels must laugh to see this spectacle. *For these people wringing their hands,* their Mission was right there, on the freeways, in the interruption, in the hurt, and at the confrontation.[1]

Playground Rules

Jesus is the master of the playground. His words and example give us a wonderful base from which to build our playground rules.

Playground Rule #1—Don't throw stones. I love the first 11 verses of John chapter 8. This is the story of the woman caught in adultery being brought to Jesus for condemnation. What a scene this must have been. Here is a woman, in who knows what state of dress, dragged before Jesus by a bunch of religious men who had probably been lying in wait or perhaps even set a trap for her simply to test Jesus on his moral code. (I always wonder where the other half of this adulterous set-up was, but that's another issue.) I don't know who I feel most sorry for in this story. Is it the woman who is obviously humiliated, degraded, and afraid for her life? Is it Jesus who is being annoyed beyond belief by the religious men who still have no clue what he's really all about? Or do I pity most the people who think it's appropriate to humiliate another person to make a religious point?

Jesus lays down a very important Playground Rule when he replies, in response to an entrapping question, that anyone who has never done anything wrong in his life can begin the punishment decreed for this woman. He may cast the first stone. The oldest folks walk away first because they know what they've done in their many years of life. Then the rest start to leave. Finally nobody is left but Jesus and the woman. And Jesus saves her—twice. Not only does he save her from condemnation and death, he saves her for a life that is now a clean slate. He saves her so she can choose to make her life better, more in keeping with what God had in mind for her. He invites her, "Go now and leave your life of sin."

On life's playground, put down the rocks of condemnation and encourage people to be the best they can be, which always has as its foundation in living fully in God's love.

Playground Rule #2—Have plenty of water on hand. Water is something we all need. In a similar way, we all need encouragement and love. Be on the lookout for the small but consistent things you can do for others that help them stay healthy and nourished. Smile, touch, hug, express appreciation for everyday things, compliment traits that may not be headline news but make the atmosphere better or the load lighter. Jesus said of living life in his steps, "This is a large work I've called you into, but don't be overwhelmed by it. It's best to start small. Give a cool cup of water to someone who is thirsty, for instance. The smallest act of giving or receiving makes you a true apprentice" (Matthew 10:42 MSG).

Playground Rule #3—Don't keep score. Kids are masters at keeping score. They want the slices of cake to be even. They want to know their siblings have brushed their teeth if they themselves have had to do so. They are very interested in the chores being evenly distributed. Adults are this way, too.

We're just more sophisticated in how we ensure the score is even.

Jesus told his Sermon-on-the-Mount listeners in Matthew 5:41, "If someone forces you to go one mile, go with him two miles." He was referring to the common practice of Roman soldiers forcing the common people to carry things for them. He was suggesting that the kingdom of God is populated by people who don't keep score and who use every situation to live outrageously big-heartedly. Eugene Peterson, in his translation The Message, puts the same passage this way: "And if someone takes unfair advantage of you, use the occasion to practice the servant life. No more tit-for-tat stuff. Live generously."

Playground Rule #4—Play hide and seek. I once had the opportunity to go to Disney World on a business trip with a company for whom I was a sales trainer. I learned something very interesting about a particular type of Disney park employee. Disney employs individuals for the sole purpose of looking for crying children and giving them a sticker or other little token to help them cheer up. When my family joined me a few days later, I saw this concept in action. During a walk down the main street of MGM, my daughter, Madison, who was six at the time, was crying because we weren't purchasing a hat she wanted. Sure enough, nearly out of the woodwork came this costumed starlet wannabe who invited Madison to sit down on a bench with her. Once they were seated, the starlet handed Madison a play $100 bill and told her to buy herself a smile. The only job this starlet did for the Disney company was to seek out and find crying children and help them feel better. Jesus said of himself, "The Son of Man came to seek and to save what was lost" (Luke 19:10).

We should be ever ready to play two kinds of hide and seek. One: Look for those who are truly lost. These are the sheep, the people who don't know God. They have not yet been introduced to God's outlandish love, or they have continually chosen not to believe it for themselves. We need to keep seeking and finding and sharing God's love with these people.

Two: Look for those who know God but who need an affirmation that calls them into a deeper relationship with him. These folks know about God, may believe God exists, may even embrace the title of Christian, but they get lost in the everyday rush of things to do, money to make, people to tend, or places to go. They are lost because they may be using activity to mask that they don't truly recognize and receive God's love. (And, consequently, they don't honestly deeply love themselves.)

We are to look for those who are in need of a good word or healing touch. Bring out the best in others.

Playground Rule #5—People are always more important than rules. I think this was the problem my kindergarten teacher was identifying in me when she said I was bossy. I thought the rules must be obeyed at any cost and made it my business to patrol the kindergarten ensuring everyone toed the line.

In his earthly life, Jesus wasn't all that happy or impressed with people like me. He said, "Woe to you, teachers of the law and Pharisees, you hypocrites! You give a tenth of your spices—mint, dill and cummin. But you have neglected the more important matters of the law—justice, mercy and faithfulness. You should have practiced the latter, without neglecting the former. You blind guides! You strain out a gnat but swallow a camel" (Matthew 23:23-24).

For my money, one of the most unsung heroes of Scripture is Joseph, the earthly father of Jesus. Long before his son was old enough to teach him this playground rule, Joseph was practicing this fundamental call. When he found out his fiancée was pregnant before he had marital relations with her, he could have had Mary humiliated and stoned to death at her parents' doorway. Instead, Joseph opted to mesh righteousness with mercy and simply have her "put away," which means he would have broken the engagement but not made a big deal out of the reason. He knew people were more important than rules. And his heart was ready to hear from the angel the absolutely remarkable news of his betrothed and her role in spiritual history. God can talk more clearly to people who understand this playground rule.

On the playground of life, it's the justice we seek for those who are oppressed and victimized, it's the mercy we extend to those in need of earthly goods or spiritual comfort, and it's the faithfulness we exhibit to our relationships that are the real tests of what our faith is all about, not how well we keep the rules. Jesus encourages us to keep the rules as much as we can, all the while attending to the more important facets of life such as justice, mercy, and faithfulness. If your rule-keeping comes first, you may be in playground violation.

Playground Rule #6 — Don't call names. Jesus' language was pretty strong when he addressed name callers. When he got wind of the fact that some of the people in his community were calling each other "fool," he cautioned them that they could be in danger of the fire of hell (Matthew 5:22).

Name-calling is dangerous for three reasons. First, when we call someone a name, we signal we are angry. As long as we are name-calling, there is little chance of reconciliation. Being angry isn't necessarily a problem, but being angry enough to call names may signal a heart that is not yet willing to forgive.

Second, depending on who we are calling the name, we are in danger of them believing us and beginning to act in the way that we label them. Children and people over whom we have authority may be particularly vulnerable to this danger. They may believe us when we call them stupid, lazy, or rebellious, and decide to fulfill those roles.

Third, name-calling is disrespectful to God's creation. I believe that's what grieved Jesus most about people calling each other names. Jesus knew when we did this we were depersonalizing someone, we were disparaging the image of

God in that person. We also hurt ourselves in that we separate ourselves from the heart of God, the heart that loves us and the other person deeply.

She Plays Well with Others

One Sunday as I was getting ready for church, I wrestled with two options for the morning. There were two places I could be in the church building. As I pondered my decision, it seemed to me the Holy Spirit whispered in my ear, "Go to the sanctuary. I'll meet you there with a surprise." Talk about an offer I couldn't refuse!

Not knowing at all what to expect, I went to the sanctuary where I met a beautiful young woman named Anna Edwards, who told the story of God's call on her life and how she had answered him. I was so moved by her remarkable obedience to the third Call for All—love others—that I asked her if I could share her story. She graciously said yes.

> Some people describe their calling as a specific moment when they know exactly what God has intended for them to do. Mine was a little different. I grew up in church and knew full well that to those whom much is given, much is expected. I always wanted to be more involved in missions but never thought I had enough time. God told me what a poor excuse this was, so I worked hard, graduated early, and took a year to focus on his plans for my life. With a little work and digging, the perfect opportunity opened up for me in a homeless shelter in Maryland, seeking out the lost and hungry and caring for them as God would care for his lost children.
>
> I packed my car and drove to Earleville, a farming community with a population smaller than my home congregation (4,200). Every day presented its own excitement, blessings, challenges, and opportunities to grow closer to Christ in a mission of reconciliation as described in 2 Corinthians 5.

This homeless shelter is unique in that it is set on a beautiful farm 15 miles away from the nearest small town. About a dozen chickens, a lamb, a goat, several cats, Elvis the hound dog, and 35 men, women, and children call Clairvaux Farm their home. You see, most people support the ideas of shelters, but they don't want them in their backyard.

I was an all-purpose volunteer, and I found myself doing a wide variety of activities to help the shelter operate smoothly. I drove a van into town twice a week to go to Social Services, doctors' appointments, Wal-Mart runs, to look for housing, or just to allow people some time off the farm. I served the role of "truck driver," driving all over Maryland, Delaware, and parts of Pennsylvania to pick up donations that ranged from furniture to food donations. When the need arose, I would box food for people who would drive up looking for help. Because the coordinator of the shelter, Bobby, was blind, I was in charge of administering the drug tests. At one point, he was sick in the hospital and left me in charge for a few days. When, as if I weren't nervous enough with the responsibility of watching over 40 people, one of the ladies called the police on another resident. I found myself sorting out death threats and reports of child abuse, wondering how a college degree in Religious Studies could have prepared me for a situation such as this.

But all of these things were just work that I did that kept me busy; I believe my mission was more than that. I went to Maryland to love as Christ loved. If there is anyone in this world who needs love, a homeless person is at the top of the list. I did not really understand that oftentimes the demons that these people face have a tendency to drive away friends and family members. Bobby taught me how to love as we are commanded to love. So I did. And Christ opened my heart to learn to love alcoholics, addicts, a murderer, a father who molested his handicapped daughter, and a prostitute spreading AIDS.

I think I received far more than I could give. Bobby, in his blindness, had the ability to look past what you and I might first judge a person for. He could see into the soul. He had a way of knowing people more as I believe God would know them. I learned more about life and human nature in four months than I did during any of my schooling up to this point. Wonderfully amazing people welcomed me into their lives, shared their stories, and blessed me with trust and friendship.

God sent me into the world, showed me his lost sheep, and taught me how to serve them. This required an element of trust—trust in God to provide me with the skills and talents to be able to overcome the many social barriers between a young, naïve college student and weathered veterans of the streets and woods. I had to trust God to open the hearts of all of us.

Now, I grant you, Anna faced an extreme playground, interacting with people who are very challenging and intensely demanding on the people-skills barometer. But if Anna can play well with these folks, can understand that the last of the three calls for all is to love others fully, we can each think of our own surroundings and how we might do the same.

The Ultimate Parent

I wonder if God-the-Parent ever gets exasperated with all of us in the same way I sometimes get exasperated with my own two kids. You know the drill. One of them pushes the other, sometimes in just a very small way to not be detected by me. But the other one yelps and pushes back. Then a few unkind names are said, and the escalation begins. When it becomes obvious they aren't going to stop this on their own and the volume gets high and a flesh wound seems imminent, I strongly suggest, "Be nice." It's the best advice I can give at the time. Sometimes the simplest, most succinct idea is the best one. Be a decent, generous, nice human being to your fellow human beings—*all* of them, not just the ones who are easy to love. Play nicely with each other. Live out Paul's advice to his friends in Ephesus:

> As a prisoner for the Lord, then, I urge you to live a life worthy of the calling you have received. Be completely humble and gentle; be patient, bearing with one another in love. Make every effort to keep the unity of the Spirit through the bond of peace. There is one body and one Spirit—just as you were called to one hope when you were called—one Lord, one faith, one baptism; one God and Father of all, who is over all and through all and in all (Ephesians 4:1-6).

Playing nicely is a lot easier when we have answered the previous two calls to receive God's outlandish love and to thoroughly love ourselves. We are then filled to overflowing with the goodness it takes to answer this third call for all of us—to love others.

Moving to Deeper Space

When we answer the Call for All—love God, love ourselves, love others—our lives will feel full, fresh, and productive. We will be very active people. But our hearts long for something more. We yearn for our very own personal purpose—our unique Divine Assignment. So while filling these three basic calls makes for a peaceful, purposeful life, we're not done yet.

The Divine Assignment that we are going to explore in the rest of this book will never be enough for us if the foundation of receiving and responding to God's love, loving ourselves as God loves us, and playing well with others isn't laid. But the Divine Assignment will bring us deep satisfaction when we seek to live it in conjunction with the Call for All. The foundation needs to be strong for the house to be sound. So make sure your foundation is durable, then get ready for more exploration, discovery, and construction.

Discovering More About You

1. Where have you recently been tempted to condemn someone else but realized you had done the same thing yourself?

2. What are you critical about in other people that may also be a temptation for you?

3. Who in your life needs someone to come looking for them? How can you effectively communicate God's love to someone who needs to know about it?

4. How can you use your talents and influence to change to good a particular situation you may be facing at this point?

5. Where would you place yourself on an importance spectrum that has as its two ends "people" or "rules"? Why? Is there ever a time when rules are more important than people? How do rules serve people and not the other way around?

6. Is there a situation in which you would like to seek revenge? How else can it be resolved? Can you trust God's timing for the outcome?

7. Who is sick, hurting, or fallen in your life? How can you be an agent of God's grace to them?

8. Ask God how he wants you to play more nicely with others. Write his response.

❧

*D*ear God,

Forgive me for believing that playing well with others is an optional call. I know there are specialized ways each of us live out this call, but it's a call for all of us, just the same.

Lord, help me to remember that you always give me a call like this with the promise that I will never be given more than I can handle. You walk beside me every day to help me as I help others.

Make me more aware of the ways my life and your heart can make a difference. Give me eyes to see and ears to hear. Give me courage and confidence as I become more aware of your playground rules and how I can more effectively live within them.

Thank you for Jesus, whose masterful examples of living the playground rules gives me a model for my behavior and my character. Through his life and his words, I have been given plenty to keep me busy as I seek to become more like him in how I interact with all the other remarkable creatures you have put on this earth.

In Christ's name, amen.

Part 2

Pinpointing Your Purpose

❧

Every human is intended to have a character of his own,
to be what no others are and to do what no others can do.
WILLIAM ELLERY CHANNING

FIVE

The Personal Archeological Dig

❧

Learn what you are and be such.

PINDAR

Ah, you say, now we're getting down to the reason I picked up this book in the first place! For even with the three distinct calls on our lives—love God, love ourselves, love others—we long for something more personalized for ourselves. We want a sense of our individual significance and purpose. We want a specialized reason for being that sets us apart from everyone else. The apostle Paul gave great advice to his friends in Galatia:

> Live creatively, friends....Make a careful exploration of who you are and the work you have been given, and then sink yourself into that. Don't be impressed with yourself. Don't compare yourself with others. Each of you must take responsibility for doing the creative best you can with your own life (Galatians 6:1,4-5 MSG).

At the magnificent Children's Museum of Indianapolis, there is a fun exhibit on the lower level that replicates an archeological dig of dinosaur bones. Kids enter the exhibit once they have put on goggles. They use little scraping tools and small soft paintbrushes to do their part in the excavation process. The museum doesn't give the kids pick axes and dynamite to uncover the treasure. Using such forceful and large-scale tools would certainly damage or completely wipe out the intricate riches waiting to be uncovered and celebrated. Likewise, each of us is a rich resource waiting to be excavated. But the mining needs to be done gently, respectfully, and over time. The most important thing to remember in this process is that it is exactly that—a process. Sometimes we make large leaping discoveries, but more often we hear the still, small voice that speaks a glimpse of deeper understanding. Sometimes we make big changes based on what we uncover, but more often we will gradually grow in grace and be transformed into the unique expression of God we are each meant to be.

What Are We Looking For?

What are the marks of a unique Divine Assignment?

1. *A stretching*—God will never give you a Divine Assignment you can handle by yourself. Where would be the fun in that for him? God's hopes and dreams for you include a close, unbroken, and dynamic relationship with him. The divine call he places on your life will always initially leave you saying, "I can't do this by myself." No, of course not. God's greatest plans for you are to be with him so that *together* you accomplish something. He knows that any other arrangement has the potential to leave you frustrated or, even worse, conceited.

2. *A healing for you*—This aspect of the Divine Assignment, especially the two-word particular purpose, is absolutely critical to understand and embrace. God loves you so much that he planted a need and a desire in your heart for the world that would first need to be satisfied in you. For example, my friend

Laura discovered her particular purpose to be "Encourage Kindness." God gave that purpose to Laura because she suffered some setbacks as a child that no young child should have to endure. But she did. And as she grew to be an adult, for her life to become more nourished and healed, she needed to experience kindness. In God's great wisdom, he planted in her the seed of this longing so he could show her how much the world needs kindness, starting with herself. God's hope and dream for Laura was that she know and understand kindness fully, first by being kind to herself so she could then spread it authentically to others. God cares about you first—as if you were the only person on earth.

My particular purpose is to "Stimulate Wisdom." God knew that my weakness is being foolish, listening to the voices of the culture, straying off the path on a regular basis. God knew that for my life to be whole, I would need to have a central focus on wisdom—to learn all I could about wisdom, to apply it in every aspect of my life, and to have the opportunity to want wisdom for others. But God had to heal me first before I could heal others. I have to stimulate wisdom in myself before I can genuinely ask others to join me.

I witness this powerful reality at the end of every semester I teach at the local community college. I have the privilege of teaching psychology and sociology to students who come from all over the city, are as diverse as they can be, and many of whom are attending school against all odds. I deeply admire these people.

The assignment they are to complete at the end of the term is to choose any subject we have covered and dive more deeply into the topic. Often the students will choose something that has affected them personally such as divorce, abuse, infidelity, alcoholism, or a chronic mental or physical health problem. As they give their reports, I'm struck over and over with the passion they embody as they are telling the rest of the class about their topic. God has given them a zeal for their topic that is part of what has healed them. Time and again I have suggested they turn that healing into advocacy or a need to educate and liberate others caught in situations they have grown out of.

Our Divine Assignments are sent to us, along with the circumstances that have brought it into being, to heal us, to restore us, to make us more empathically human. As you start to put together your own particular purpose, you will find a word or two that seem to encapsulate what you long for and need most. Those words are the very messengers of God's unique plan for your wholeness, of him making all things new—including and starting with you!

3. *A healing for others*—Have you ever been around people who made you feel better by being in their presence? Their easy air of unself-conscious confidence gave you encouragement to relax and be yourself. Or their passion for life and what they were and did gave you renewed enthusiasm and vision. Maybe these people simply listened and let you work out something you had on your mind and heart, and you felt better in their presence just because they knew what to say and what not to say.

Chances are excellent they were living their Divine Assignments.

When you realize and begin to live your Assignment, you will become such a person to others. They will find benefit and healing just being around you, even if you're not "doing" anything. Have you ever had someone say to you "Thank you so much" and your response was "But I didn't do anything"? Chances are excellent you were living your Divine Assignment. People will be healed by God through you just being and doing what God meant you to be and do, not by all the things you may think you should be and do to benefit the world.

4. *A guarantee of a dynamic life*—One of the most frequently asked questions about a Divine Assignment is "Does it change over time?" No and yes.

Once you articulate your particular Divine Assignment, you can look back over your life and see that it's been functioning throughout your life when you were at your best. The essence of who you are and your deep-seated values and passions don't tend to change a lot over time. Personality psychologists tell us our traits and characteristics are often very stable.[1]

What does change are circumstances, relationships, and our own freedom in expressing ourselves as we grow older and more sure of who we are. When we look at chapter 9 regarding relationships and chapter 10 on tasks, you'll see how your Divine Assignment can play out in a number of situations. As most of us are very aware, our essence may not change, but our circumstances do with startling regularity.

5. *A heart inscription*—As we go on our "archeological" dig, we stay mindful that our hearts need to be focused on their proper responsibility, which is to stay in close communication with the Holy Spirit. It's always amazing to me when people of faith won't trust their hearts, always fearing that their flesh may be steering them wrong. But Scripture is very clear. If we center the intention of our hearts on God, we can then trust our hearts to understand God's guidance

It's also helpful to note that the word "heart" in Hebrew is also translated as "will." So as we are willing to place ourselves in God's care and control, we are keeping ourselves and our hearts moving in the right direction. If our intentions are continually and increasingly becoming aligned with God, we are on the right track. One of the most beautiful assurances of this fact is in Philippians 4:4-7:

> Rejoice in the Lord always. I will say it again: Rejoice! Let your gentleness be evident to all. The Lord is near. Do not be anxious about anything, but in everything, by prayer and petition, with thanksgiving, present your requests to God. And the peace

of God, which transcends all understanding, will guard your hearts and your minds in Christ Jesus.

We also learn from Scripture that God writes on our hearts—he inscribes on them his words, intentions, and desires:

> "This is the covenant I will make with the house of Israel after that time," declares the LORD. "I will put my law in their minds and write it on their hearts. I will be their God, and they will be my people. No longer will a man teach his neighbor, or a man his brother saying, 'Know the LORD,' because they will all know me, from the least of them to the greatest,'" declares the LORD (Jeremiah 31:33-34).

> Now what I am commanding you today is not too difficult for you or beyond your reach. It is not up in heaven, so that you have to ask, "Who will ascend into heaven and get it and proclaim it to us so we may obey it?" Nor is it beyond the sea, so that you have to ask, "Who will cross the sea to get it and proclaim it to us so we may obey it?" No, the word is very near you; it is in your mouth and in your heart so you may obey it (Deuteronomy 30:11-14).

Isn't it funny how many other places we look for God's hopes and longings for us? We look everywhere but within ourselves. God tries to make it as easy as possible for us to know our Divine Assignments. It's in our hearts.

Once we have made the transition to our awareness that we are children of God, the most powerful influence over our hearts or our wills is given to us:

> Because you are sons, God sent the Spirit of his Son into our hearts, the Spirit who calls out, "*Abba,* Father." So you are no longer a slave, but a son; and

since you are a son, God has made you also an heir
(Galatians 4:6).

As we stay centered, we can trust that what we're "hearing"
is what God has written on each of our hearts for us to understand and act upon.

6. *A fit*—One of the groundbreakers in the "purpose" rev-
olution is a brilliant and engaging woman named Laurie Beth
Jones. She wrote *The Path* and taught a seminar by the same
name. One quality Laurie Beth has as she speaks in her sem-
inars is the lovely ability to enable her participants to see
Scripture in a new and refreshing light. She brings the Word
alive. Her understanding of this next passage brought great
clarity to me as I enjoyed being her student one weekend:

> Come to me, all you who are weary and burdened,
> and I will give you rest. Take my yoke upon you and
> learn from me, for I am gentle and humble in
> heart, and you will find rest for your souls. For my
> yoke is easy and my burden is light (Matthew 11:28-
> 30).

Laurie Beth does a masterful job of setting the stage for
this passage. Here is a carpenter talking to normal people
about something he knows is very important to those
people—the yoke of their oxen. Jesus, as a carpenter, knew of
the supreme importance of a well-fitting yoke for oxen. If the
yoke was too loose, it would chafe and irritate the oxen. If the
yoke was too tight, it would strangle them. Each ox had a spe-
cially fitted yoke for maximum comfort, which translated into
maximum performance.

As Jesus likened his hopes and visions for us to the yoke
used for the oxen, he was indicating that these hopes and
visions would fit us perfectly. They were designed for us. Not
only will they fit us, but we will also find joy and satisfaction
in what we're doing. We will feel proud of our work. I used to

think this was sort of self-serving, but my friend Sara reminded me of this beautiful piece of wisdom literature:

> Then I realized that it is good and proper for a man to eat and drink, and to find satisfaction in his toilsome labor under the sun during the few days of life God has given him—for this is his lot. Moreover, when God gives any man wealth and possessions, and enables him to enjoy them, to accept his lot and be happy in his work—this is a gift of God. He seldom reflects on the days of his life, because God keeps him occupied with gladness of heart (Ecclesiastes 5:18-20).

Now, like the oxen, we still have to work. But the work and the resources fit us perfectly. That's God's grace.

7. *A confirmation of what you've known all along*—I wish I had a nickel for every time I have had the privilege of witnessing people articulate their emerging understanding of their Divine Assignments. Tears spring to their eyes as their souls seem to say, "I've wanted that to come to the surface for so long. I have known this all along, but didn't know how to say it. But now I've said it out loud, and it feels good to declare who I am."

Debbie was in a weekly group I had in my home one semester for book study. Part of the study was to get a greater understanding of each woman's Divine Assignment. For several months, Debbie kept getting closer and closer, but she seemed to be keeping the full reality at bay. One day I knew in my heart it was time to push for a little more clarity and a bit more ownership of what she knew was lurking under the surface. As she was fully supported by the others in the group, she was able to say what she knew she was being called to do as an individual. Once she got it to the surface, she felt better. She received advice and suggestions from the group on how to continue to pursue her assignment. There is power that is sometimes cataclysmic in speaking into time and space what you've only let swirl in your heart and head up to that point. Sometimes we find it's not as scary as we feared; sometimes it brings up new concerns. But once it is out in the open, it can be celebrated, mulled over, and supported by those around you who have your very best interests at heart.

What Your Divine Assignment Is Not

Here are a few things your Divine Assignment is not designed to be.

1. *Your identity*—Your identity is being a child of God. That's the bottom line. Your identity is a beloved creation nurtured and redeemed by the grace of a loving Creator. Any time we begin to put our trust in our jobs, our relationships, our purposes, or our occupations, we will be ultimately disappointed. I have decorated my office to remind me of a Tuscan grape arbor. I did this so I would always be reminded of Christ's very reassuring words:

> I am the vine; you are the branches. If a man remains in me and I in him, he will bear much fruit; apart from me you can do nothing. If anyone does not remain in me, he is like a branch that is thrown away and withers; such branches are picked up, thrown into the fire and burned. If you remain in me and my words remain in you, ask whatever you wish, and it will be given you. This is to my Father's glory, that you bear much fruit, showing yourselves to be my disciples (John 15:5-8).

I find this reassuring because I don't have to even pay attention to my own branchhood or to the fruit I'm producing. My job is to stay connected to God. My purpose will never be my salvation. That's through the one who gave me a purpose.

2. *A job or a relationship*—Your Divine Assignment will *never* be dependent on your circumstances. Relationships, even the most long-term covenantal relationships, will pass. Goodness knows in our economy and corporate culture, jobs come and go. So we should never look at our externals to give us a sense of mission. Our Divine Assignments influence the way we live out our relationships. The resources we have to carry out our Divine Assignments may be powerful influences on our jobs or careers. But our sense of God-given purpose is always about who we're called to be in a variety of situations.

The reason is obvious. If my purpose has to do with being a mother, what happens to my sense of purpose when my kids leave the house? If my purpose has to do with being married, what happens if my husband dies or leaves me? More people are left high and dry on this purpose scale because they falsely believed their identities were in their relationships.

When it comes to careers and jobs, if our purpose is embedded in position, status, or activity, what happens if we are downsized, pink-slipped, or need to retire? Or what happens if you're like me and leave your career to become a full-time stay-at-home mother? The number of people who sink into depression because of a shift in their career identity gives us a cause for pause before sinking our sense of self into our work life.

Neither relationships nor careers are the essence of our Divine Assignments, but our Divine Assignments have a profound impact on both.

3. *Grandiose or earth-shattering*—Your Divine Assignment doesn't have to change the world. In fact, it may be that your call sets the stage for others to do what they do best. John the Baptist knew in his heart that he was to decrease so that Jesus could increase. The writer of Hebrews gives a lengthy account of all the biblical characters who didn't necessarily see the fruition of their passions, but they made significant

contributions to spiritual history. My husband has a wonderful way of keeping our life participation in perspective:

> Every kindness, every beneficial involvement, every act of giving is like a stone that is tossed in a pond. Though it may be a long time before we see any visible evidence that our input is making any difference, one day we will see the confirmation of our contributions poking through the surface as, under the visible, the acts have piled up on one another gradually bringing them to the level where the eye can now see. We can never be discouraged by what we do not see, as long as we are being faithful.

4. *A luxury*—Discovering your particular Divine Assignment is not a luxury saved only for those who have time to think about these things. Someone may argue, "I don't have time for this Divine Assignment stuff. I have a family to feed. I work long hours. I have responsibilities." Or another might say, "I am overwhelmed by taking care of my elderly parents and my young children at the same time. I don't have the extravagance of finding out what is supposed to be giving me meaning in this life."

Life is demanding, rushed, and overwhelming sometimes. That's exactly why we need to know who we are and why we are on earth. If we don't, we can get depressed or exasperated. We miss the whole point of Jesus saying, "I have come that you might have life and have it abundantly." Knowing our Divine Assignment keeps us ever-mindful that God has a specific reason for us being where we are at exactly this point of history. Because the Divine Assignment is primarily about who we *are*, it helps us understand our personality and character that God wants to bring to our families, our work, and our everyday interactions with people we meet or influence.

5. *Spiritual ATM*—Discovering your Divine Assignment is not like driving up to the ATM machine, putting in a card,

and having a piece of paper spit out for you to read, tuck in your wallet, and drive away. Transformation takes exploration and experimentation. Don't be in such a hurry to get on with your purpose that you miss the growth that awaits you in diving more deeply into self-awareness, self-understanding, and self-acceptance. Transformation requires time. But you are a lot closer than you think because you have picked up this book!

Your Divine Assignment will definitely be life-changing for you.

Tools for Digging

There are four tools we will use for our "archeological" dig into our God-given purpose.

Your personal definition of success—In teaching a short segment on stress relief to a group of college students, I came across this pithy and highly insightful quote: "One of the worst reasons to follow a particular path in life is that other people want you to." Our lives are full of input from people, from those who are intimately connected with us to those who couldn't care less about us except to have us spend our money on their products. This input can have our best interests at heart or this input can seek to lead us in directions that are servicing the person who is giving us the input.

Success is measured on many different levels, including your physical health, your financial responsibility, your relationships, your contribution to your work and community, your spiritual vitality. In each of those arenas, God has planted in you your own personal definition of success. Those definitions are there to guide you along the paths he has designed specifically for you. Take some time and come up with your own personal definitions. If you are holding on to someone else's definitions, be they as close and intimate as immediate family or as impersonal as media advertising, you will be out of sync with the reason God uniquely designed you to be at this particular place on the planet in this particular period of history.

Your understanding of your beliefs—The way you believe powerfully shapes your attitudes, which in turn shape your behaviors. What do you, at the very core of your being, believe? What do you believe, not because you have been taught or conditioned to believe it, but because you know in your heart of hearts that it is true? When you write down what you truly believe, you can get a clearer picture of who you are. These can be very profound and deep beliefs or light and whimsical beliefs. They can be beliefs you would die for or beliefs that wouldn't be worth getting a black eye over.

For example, I deeply hold the belief that God's Holy Spirit is with me every hour of every day and night. What does this say about me? I'm a person who treasures the notion that there is more to life than what I can experience with my senses. I value my spiritual nature and the connection I have to the Creator God. That's a belief over which I will not be easily swayed.

I also whimsically believe that making rubber-stamped cards is the most relaxing thing I can do when it comes to crafting. What this says about me as a person is that I love color, texture, playing with paper, and making something out of nothing. It's a firm belief, but I'm not going to get into a fight about it with someone who believes differently.

Our beliefs tell us what we hold important. Some beliefs are rather universal, and some are more personal opinion. But all of them tell us something about ourselves that we need to listen to as we search for our particular purpose.

Your personal alphabet—In the book of Proverbs, we find a woman who may be a bit annoying to some of us, but someone from whom all of us—men and women, young and old—can learn about wisdom. When we get a clearer understanding of how and why Proverbs 31 was written, we can breathe a little sigh of relief if we've been comparing ourselves to her and learn some wonderful new insights about ourselves if we are wise.

The heart of Proverbs 31, the description of the woman of noble virtue, was written in poetic form using a method often used by Hebrew poets of the day. They wrote the letters of the alphabet down the side of a page, then filled in words that started with the corresponding letters to construct their poem. The poem was a combination of the universal form and the specific topic being written of.

So for this part of your excavation, you will get a sheet of paper, write our English alphabet from A to Z down the side of the paper, and fill in the words that describe you starting with each letter. These words can be interests you have, passions, causes you love, character traits, talents, or skills. You may want to refer back to the exercise on the 10 personality traits you did in chapter 3 to get some ideas about words you would like to use to describe yourself. The only thing these words can't be is negative.

At times, someone who is going through this process with me will protest that they can't think of anything or there's nothing good they can say. They may just be acting falsely modest or protesting out of a misplaced sense of humility. But if someone won't participate because they just won't acknowledge the good in themselves, I challenge them to take it up with the Creator. If we can't or won't articulate what is good and positive about ourselves, we're telling God he did a lousy job or that he made a mistake in placing us here. Julia Cameron, artist and author, says this of the power of recognizing our positive points:

> So often we are focused on what we would like to change—and change for the better—that we fail to celebrate what is wonderfully enjoyable just the way it is. We are often far closer to our ideal—and ideals—than we dare to recognize. Self-esteem is

an active choice, not a sudden given. We can choose to actively esteem our many positive traits. By counting our blessings we can come to see that we are blessed and that we need not compare ourselves to anyone.[2]

Your deep gladness and your understanding of the world's deep need—Fredrick Buechner, in his often-cited quote on vocation said, "The place God calls you to is the place where your deep gladness and the world's deep need meet." The fourth excavation tool you will use in clearing your heart and mind for discovering and implementing your particular purpose is to discern your deep gladness in this world and your understanding of this world's deep need.

When seeking your deep gladness, think back to times when you have felt profoundly satisfied or when your heart resonated with what you were experiencing in a sense that said, "This is what life is supposed to be like." A woman I had in a group one time described her experience as a young girl when someone in her neighborhood needed help. Her family stopped the car on the way to church to help the little girl, and Krista thought to herself, "This is life at its best. This is the way things are meant to be." As we mined that experience for her, she began to see the notes running through her life that kept playing the same melody. She was moved by kindness. She was deeply glad when kindness was carried out in the world.

In the same way, to uncover your particular understanding of the world's deep need, ask yourself this fill-in-the-blank question: If there was more _____ in this world, it would be a much better place. Don't rush your answer. Put some thought into it. From your unique perspective, what would make the world a better place?

One of the most beautiful realities of doing this exercise with the many people I've had the privilege to lead through the process is that everyone has a different idea about what should be in that blank. The beauty of this reality is that each of us is expressing a different characteristic of God. When we articulate our beliefs for what the world deeply needs, and we put them all together, and we help each other accomplish them instead of wondering why in the world someone else thinks that way, we bring the kingdom of God to earth as it is in heaven. The people of God are then doing what the people of God should do best—representing God in his fullness to the world that deeply needs him. None of us has all of God's traits, but buried inside each of us is at least one that God wants us to champion to make the world more complete.

Excavation Benefits

Your archeological excavation is the first step in articulating and claiming what you believe is important. You are identifying who you are and what makes you unique. This information will give you the foundation you need to recognize and name the two key words you'll be looking for in the next two chapters—your Central Passion and Greatest Strength.

Discovering More About You

1. Describe a time when you felt called by God to do something that seemed out of your comfort zone or ability level. What was your relationship with God like during the time you were carrying out the task? What did God show you about himself in the whole adventure?

2. What does it mean to you that your particular purpose is a healing for you first? What needs to be healed in your life in order for you to move out and more effectively contribute to and minister to others?

3. Life is most exciting when...

4. How do you respond to the notion that your particular purpose will fit you? Does this go against any prior teaching you have had that you will need to suffer to do God's will? How would you reconcile Jesus' declaration that he came so we would have abundant life with Jesus' declaration that we need to take up our cross?

5. What have you suspected about yourself all along that might now be coming to the surface? Think in terms of personality traits, gifts, and skills, as well as passions and interests. Write down anything, regardless of how crazy or out of character it might be for you. Your heart needs to bypass your head sometimes for a complete "you" to emerge.

6. What is your personal definition of success? Include the following categories: financial, material, social, spiritual, relational, physical, intellectual, and mental/emotional.

7. Record some of your beliefs and what they say about you. On one half of the page write "My Belief Is" and on the other side write "And This Says About Me." To start, write two serious and two whimsical answers. As more come to the surface, write them fully for maximum excavation benefit.

8. Write the letters of our alphabet down the side of a page. Write at least one character trait, gift, interest, or skill you have to correspond to the letters. If you are having trouble saying anything nice about yourself, stop, take a deep inhale and exhale, and ask God where the barrier is and how he might want to change your heart and your mind about yourself.

9. What do you feel is the world's deepest need? What do
   you feel is your greatest happiness?

10. Ask God what he wants you to specifically learn from
    the excavation tools you've used in this chapter. Write
    his answer.

§§

*A*lmighty God,
     *I am indeed fearfully and wonderfully made. There
is a lot to me! Help me grasp this reality and be appre-
ciative of all you have made me to be and to do.*
     *As I start to uncover my true self, give me the grace
to accept the positive and to be realistic about what I
might perceive to be negative. The only way I can really
get to my Divine Assignment is through a willingness
to be honest about and receptive to all you are calling
me to be and to do.*
     *I'm so excited about what I'm learning. Life with
you is never dull. Thank you.*
                         In Christ's name, amen.

SIX

Why on Earth
Are You Here?

❧

When you carry out acts of kindness you get a feeling inside.
It is as though something inside your body responds
and says, "Yes, this is how I ought to feel."

HAROLD KUSHNER

an two words change your life? You bet.

In the next two chapters, you are going to discover two powerful words that, when put in combination, will give you laser focus as to why you are here on this earth. You will discover your unique particular purpose, your Divine Assignment.

Why only two words? Because life goes fast! Not only in the number of days we have to be alive, but in the speed with which each day whizzes by. Some mornings when I wake up, I have to remind myself who I am and why I'm here. Two words are about all I can manage. Some days when life is going quickly and I get so distracted, having just two words can center my thoughts, intentions, and behaviors so I can stay on track and be a nice person at the same time. You'll write these two words on Post-it Notes, index cards, or paper of your favorite color and stick them on the bathroom mirror, car dashboard, refrigerator, computer screen, and anywhere else you are likely to see them on a regular basis. The words will help keep you grounded in your God-given identity and purpose.

The first word we'll look at is your "Central Passion." Your Central Passion is what you will uncover as you follow Paul's advice to "make a careful exploration of who you are." The second word is your "Greatest Strength," which we'll focus on in the next chapter. Together, these two words will form your Divine Assignment.

What's in a Name?

In the Bible, when God was making something happen, he sometimes changed a person's name. For instance, Genesis 17 finds two name changes that reflect the purpose God had in mind for the individuals involved:

> When Abram was ninety-nine years old, the LORD appeared to him and said, "I am God Almighty; walk before me and be blameless. I will confirm my covenant between me and you and will greatly increase your numbers." Abram fell facedown, and God said to him, "As for me, this is my covenant with you: You will be the father of many nations. No longer will you be called Abram; your name will be Abraham, for I have made you a father of many nations....
>
> God also said to Abraham, "As for Sarai your wife, you are no longer to call her Sarai; her name will be Sarah. I will bless her and will surely give you a son by her. I will bless her so that she will be the mother of nations; kings of peoples will come from her" (verses 1-5,15-16).

Another famous name change occurred in Genesis 32:22-28:

> That night Jacob got up and took his two wives, his two maidservants and his eleven sons and crossed

the ford of the Jabbok. After he had sent them across the stream, he sent over all his possessions. So Jacob was left alone, and a man wrestled with him till daybreak. When the man saw that he could not overpower him, he touched the socket of Jacob's hip so that his hip was wrenched as he wrestled with the man. The man said, "Let me go, for it is daybreak." But Jacob replied, "I will not let you go unless you bless me." The man asked him, "What is your name?" "Jacob," he answered. Then the man said, "Your name will no longer be Jacob, but Israel, because you have struggled with God and with men and have overcome."

Jacob's birth name meant "schemer" or "hustler," and he certainly proved true to his name as he hustled his older twin out of the family blessing. Israel was his "discovered" name, the name given to him based on a new identity. The identity was just beginning when he engaged in his wrestling match, but it's an identity that proved to be more true for him…and for the nation that also bears the same name.

Jesus also used a change of name when he first laid eyes on one of his soon-to-be disciples. He said, "You are Simon son of John. You will be called Cephas" (John 1:42). Cephas is translated as Peter, or "the Rock." Jesus later clarified Cephas' position after they had spent countless hours together as teacher and student and as friends:

> When Jesus came to the region of Caesarea Philippi, he asked his disciples, "Who do people say the Son of Man is?" They replied, "Some say John the Baptist; others say Elijah; and still others, Jeremiah or one of the prophets." "But what about you?" he asked. "Who do you say I am?" Simon Peter answered, "You are the Christ, the Son of the living God." Jesus replied, "Blessed are you, Simon son of Jonah, for this was not revealed to you by man, but by my Father in heaven. And I tell you

that you are Peter, and on this rock I will build my
church, and the gates of Hades will not overcome
it. I will give you the keys of the kingdom of heaven;
whatever you bind on earth will be bound in
heaven, and whatever you loose on earth will be
loosed in heaven" (Matthew 16:13-19).

Peter's full identity and specific purpose were revealed to
him once he understood who Jesus was. His name took on
increased significance and became a guiding force in his life.

Just as Abram, Sarai, Jacob, and Simon had their destinies
come into sharper focus as they encountered God more personally and intimately, your journey toward your Divine
Assignment will bring your identity into clearer view.
Abraham, Sarah, Israel, and Peter were changed and had new
names to use as a marker they could daily refer to, letting
them know God was in control and had a plan. Your Central
Passion—your "name," so to speak—clarifies your identity in
Christ and reminds you that God has a purpose for you. The
one-word Central Passion will become a touchstone you can
use when you need a booster shot of confidence that God
does indeed have hopes and dreams for you.

Zeroing in on Your Central Passion

Look back at the excavation exercises in the last chapter.
Are there some themes running through all of your discoveries? Themes are characteristics or values that seem to surface over and over again. For example, if you keep seeing
words or values like "kindness" or "justice" or "encouragement" pop up, these are themes in your life. These recurring
passions or desires will come to the forefront of your thinking
and your hopes for yourself and the world. Write down some
of the words that come to mind. Your Central Passion will be
a word that expresses the common threads of your "archeological dig" into yourself.

Look at the words you wrote down. Which ones stand out? Which words really strike chords in your heart? Now look carefully at the following list. What words are closely related to your "theme" words?

Balance	Goodness	Peace
Benevolence	Grace	Perseverance
Caring	Gratitude	Purity
Comfort	Health	Reliability
Compassion	Honesty	Responsibility
Connection	Honor	Safety
Courage	Hope	Self-worth
Creativity	Hospitality	Service
Devotion	Humor	Simplicity
Dignity	Initiative	Trust
Faith	Joy	Understanding
Faithfulness	Justice	Unity
Forgiveness	Kindness	Vitality
Freedom	Loyalty	Wellness
Generosity	Mercy	Wholeness
Gentleness	Patience	Wisdom

Now narrow your list to three words that best describe you. As you choose these words, ask yourself:

1. If I could talk about nothing else for the rest of my life, what would I want to talk about?
2. If my name were changed to one of the words in the list, what would I want to be known as?
3. What word do I want people to think of when they think of me?

After you've chosen your three words, write each one of them on a separate 3 x 5 card. Spread them out in front of you. Which one is strongest in your mind? This is your Central Passion. If none of the words in the list feels like an exact fit, but a couple are close, get out your trusty dictionary and thesaurus. Look up the words, and try on different versions until you find something that fits.

Many times people ask, "Is my Central Passion what I feel I am or is it what I'm hoping to be?" The answer is both. You already have in you a portion of your particular purpose, whether you are living it to the fullest right now or not. So you probably already recognize in yourself the kernel of the Central Passion you have been given. This process you're going through right now often brings that kernel to realization, then gives it the ground in which to grow as you recognize and give a name to that which has been lurking unnamed in your heart and mind for a long time. For example, my Central Passion is Wisdom. Now, my kids will tell you (and rightly so) that there are many days when I do not act or speak wisely. Yet wisdom is what I know I'm here to be about. It's what I'm most upset by when I see it lacking in the world, and what I'm most excited by when I see it lived out in the world. So wisdom is something I am already, and something I need to grow into more fully.

Another question that surfaces from time to time puts a real smile on my face as I answer the one who voices it. Sometimes people will ask, "What if I choose the wrong word?" I confess I more than smile; I actually giggle as I say, "Well, how much damage could you do if you initially choose 'Kindness' only to find farther down the road that it's actually 'Generosity'?"

Keep track of all the words that describe you. Although you'll only choose one from this chapter for your Central Passion and one from the next chapter for your Greatest Strength, you'll use all of the words you come up with as you craft your vision statement (in chapter 10), when you talk about your relationships with others (in chapter 8), and as you are describing the talents, skills, gifts, and character traits you have (in chapter 9).

Don't shrink back from actually participating in this exercise. Discovering your Central Passion is a *process,* and you will circle back through some of the steps several times as your receive deeper clarity from the Holy Spirit. Remember: Discovering your Central Passion is an ongoing adventure with God!

Discovering More About You

1. What themes repeatedly surfaced as you did the excavation exercises in chapter 5?

2. Like Abraham, Sarah, Israel, and Peter, how might God be bringing your identity into clearer focus?

3. What character trait or quality would you like to have people associate with you?

4. Ask God how he wants to use your Central Passion to heal you and to heal others. Write his response.

❦

Gracious and loving God,
Thank you for bringing me one step closer to the
clarity of what you have called me to be and to do.
In Christ's name, amen.

SEVEN

Your Greatest Strength

❧

The desire to fulfill the purpose for which
we were created is a gift from God.

A.W. TOZER

Your Central Passion is only half of your Divine Assignment. You also have a tremendous strength that you have probably been using all your life across many situations. An assignment usually has an element of action to it, and discerning your Greatest Strength will give you the forward momentum you need to continue discovering your Divine Assignment. Assessing your Greatest Strength is addressing the piece of Paul's puzzle that directs us to "make a careful exploration of…the work you have been given to do" (Galatians 6:1 MSG).

Your Greatest Strength is a word that embodies the activity you have most been about all your life. In fact, it's sometimes difficult for a person to come up with his greatest strength because he has been using it for so long. It's second nature. Or people may believe that because it's such an inborn strength in themselves, everyone has it. Many times I have had a client say to me, "But everyone can do *that.*" Well, honestly, not everyone can. So in this part of the transformation, we need to be discerning and a little removed from ourselves to get a greater perspective on the work we've been given to do.

To start honing in on your Greatest Strength, look through the word list below and on the next page. There are a lot of words in this list, so in the "Discovering More About You" section of this chapter, I'll tell you how to whittle it down to the few that you'll work with.

Greatest Strength Word List

Accomplish	Defend	Formulate
Achieve	Deliver	Further
Acknowledge	Demonstrate	Gather
Actualize	Describe	Generate
Administer	Design	Give
Advance	Determine	Grow
Advocate	Develop	Help
Affirm	Direct	Highlight
Aid	Discover	Host
Assess	Discuss	Identify
Awaken	Dispense	Ignite
Believe	Distribute	Illuminate
Bestow	Educate	Illustrate
Build	Embody	Impart
Call forth	Empower	Improve
Cause	Enact	Increase
Celebrate	Encourage	Infuse
Choose	Envision	Initiate
Clarify	Establish	Inspire
Communicate	Evaluate	Integrate
Compel	Explain	Invite
Confirm	Explore	Keep
Construct	Express	Kindle
Continue	Facilitate	Know
Counsel	Finance	Launch
Create	Find	Lead

Learn	Prepare	Save
Magnify	Present	Seek
Maintain	Process	Share
Make	Produce	Stand for
Manage	Promote	Stimulate
Master	Protect	Strengthen
Measure	Provide	Summon
Model	Pursue	Supervise
Mold	Radiate	Support
Monitor	Raise	Sustain
Motivate	Reclaim	Teach
Navigate	Recommend	Translate
Negotiate	Refine	Trust
Nourish	Reform	Uncover
Nurture	Relate	Understand
Open	Release	Unify
Orchestrate	Remember	Uphold
Organize	Renew	Utilize
Perform	Represent	Validate
Plan	Respect	Value
Plant	Restore	Verbalize
Practice	Reveal	Verify
Preach	Safeguard	Welcome

As you're starting to tease to the surface this Greatest Strength, consider this quote by Baltasar Gracion: "Great ability develops and reveals itself increasingly with every new assignment." Try to remember yourself in the sandbox as a child. What were you doing there? Were you directing, designing, constructing, encouraging? As you moved into school activities, to what were you drawn? Did you like research, communication, dispensing advice, organizing? In every job you've ever had, what did you find yourself doing even if it wasn't in your job description? Were you promoting, training, validating, preparing?

As I was taking myself through this exercise, I realized that I have always been trying to get people to do things, whether it was supporting a team or buying a product. I have never been content to have things be just the way they were. Any time I went into a new job, I looked around for how things could be more effective and more exciting, even if it wasn't part of my job description. As I went through the Greatest Strength list, I was continually drawn to words like motivate, generate, stimulate, celebrate. They are electrical words to me.

You may find you're drawn to quiet words, or production words, or academic words. In fact, you will quite often find your words start to cluster around central themes. Go with those themes and see which word fits the best.

Making Tough Decisions

There are a few little tricks to wading through all of the words in the Greatest Strength list.

1. If you're getting stuck, ask yourself, "Would I rather _____ or _____?"

2. Some words on the Greatest Strength list can be translated into words that go on the Central Passion list, and vice versa. For example, "encourage" can become "courage"; "communicate" can become "communication."

3. Ask people who you really trust to select one word for you. Sometimes other people who live outside our own skin can narrow things down faster than we can.

4. Remember that you will incorporate all of your words somewhere down the line as the transformation unfolds through your vision statement, your relationships, and the use of your many resources. Don't be afraid that you're going to "throw away" a wonderfully good word that you really feel describes you.

5. If you have your Central Passion nailed down, pair it with various Greatest Strengths to see what clicks. Wear each pair around for several days to see what fits.

This is a pivotal point in the discovery process, and it's not at all unusual to feel like you're overwhelmed or having a hard time settling on your words. You may just need to play with your words more, or you may have something going on inside that's keeping you from moving forward. If you're hung up on an internal hook, you need to ask yourself why you're hesitant to move into this phase of learning about yourself. Are you afraid of making a mistake? Are you wary of making a commitment? Are you concerned you won't be able to live out what you're discovering? These are potent roadblocks. If you find yourself in this situation, I recommend you move to chapter 11 to address some of the mind games we play that hinder us from moving forward.

Remember that you are not doing this on your own. God is even more excited for you to know this information than you are to know it. God can and will walk with you as you try on words and phrases. In the end, you cannot make a mistake that will be damaging or irreparable to anyone. You will not be at peace (one of God's fondest hopes and desires for you) if you stay in the middle of the road. And, of course, you can't live up to the Divine Assignment on your own. That's why you're God's *partner,* not his slave.

Putting It All Together

In putting your Central Passion and Greatest Strength words together, you will uncover your Divine Assignment. You have made a careful excavation of who you are and the work you've been given to do. This is yours. Your complete, two-word, power-packed Divine Assignment is the particular purpose of your life. Knowing this can be the start of many things making more sense in your life and putting all kinds of things in perspective. Jennifer expresses it like this:

> Working through the process of discovering my Divine Assignment has been a blessing for me in many ways. I don't like feeling "churned up" and

worried, constantly thinking about what may
happen, what I should have done, or should not
have said. Harmony is something I have always
desired and worked toward, often without realizing
it. When I actually labeled this desire as "nurturing
peace," pieces of my life's puzzle began to fall into
place, truly changing my attitudes and the way I
approach life. The little everyday annoyances no
longer bother me as they once did because I know
God is in charge.

Laurie Beth Jones challenges her mission statement seminar participants to check what they are uncovering as their
particular purpose with the following questions:

Is it you?

Is it true?

Does it excite you?

Does it excite others?

Would you be willing to have your life be about
this and only this?

Can you do this at work?

Can you do this at home?

Can you do this at a party?

Can you do this alone?

These tremendous questions clarify the understanding
that your Divine Assignment is something you apply to the
entire spectrum of your life. It's not only about work, or
family, or your own personal development. It's a transformation that touches every part of your day.

One of the mothers in a weekly group I was leading put the
Divine Assignment into moving perspective. She said, "As I get
a better handle on my Divine Assignment from God, I see how
it has been a longing in my life all along. The other wonderful
thing it has done for me is to put into perspective all of my personal suffering in the past." What she was saying is that discovering her Divine Assignment made sense to her because it was

truly a way that God could use what she had suffered and turn it to empathy and compassion for others as they were going through something similar. She could look back over the painful times in her life to see that those were building her understanding of her Central Passion and her Greatest Strength, which were helping her then be healed of those hurts while she was also making a healing contribution to her world.

Now, like a race horse snorting and pawing in the starting gates, you might be wondering what do to with all of this new-found energy born of clarified purpose. Indeed, Paul said once you know who you are and the work you've been given to do, it's time to sink yourself into it. The next part of your discovery involves how your Divine Assignment impacts your relationships and how the wonderful gifts you have been given will come into play as your transformation starts to spill over into the world, touching lives and situations. You are ready to dive more deeply into the "do" part of your particular purpose—how you're going to make a difference.

Discovering More About You

1. Write down the five Greatest Strengths, one word per each 3x5 card. Lay them out in front of you.

2. Now narrow the five down to two.

3. Which word speaks to you the most? This is your Greatest Strength.

4. Pair your Greatest Strength with your Central Passion. You now have a two-word power statement—your Divine Assignment. For example, my Central Passion is Wisdom and my Greatest Strength is Stimulate. My Divine Assignment is to Stimulate Wisdom.

Special note: If you're getting stuck, develop a Discernment Deck. If you're having trouble figuring out which words most fit you best, write your three top Central Passion words on three 3x5 cards. Write your five Greatest Strengths on five 3x5 cards. Start pairing them with each other, switching cards in combination until you find the combination that brings a light of recognition to your heart. If nothing strikes you right off the bat, try several pairs on for a few days. Remember, this is not a Divine Assignment ATM; this is the spiritual *process* of transformation. Good things take time. Once you have the two words that fit, keep the other cards. You'll be using them in the next three chapters.

5. Write your Divine Assignment: My Divine Assignment is to (Greatest Strength) (Central Passion).

6. Ask God how he feels about you. Write his response.

❧

Almighty and gracious God,

In some ways I've always known my Divine Assignment. In some ways it's a totally new revelation. Thank you that in your brilliance and love as my designer and creator, you placed these understandings in my heart so that I would know peace as I know truth. When I become more aligned with you, I feel more peaceful whatever I perceive the road to be bringing, whatever I need to accept, whatever I need to change.

This process is very exciting! Thank you for helping me discern my God-given purpose. Your love for me is truly astounding.

In Christ's name, amen.

Part 3

Living Your Divine Assignment

❧

*The real voyage of discovery consists not in
seeking new landscapes but in having new eyes.*
MARCEL PROUST

EIGHT

The Greatest Impact You'll Ever Make

❧

You should not suffer the past.
You should be able to wear it like a loose garment,
take it off and let it drop.

EVA JESSYE

We were made for relationships. Everything we are and everything we do involves interacting with others. We live in families, we interface with humans all the time in commerce. Even the most die-hard, one-person business entrepreneurs need other people to launch and maintain their businesses. We are community-oriented creatures, even those of us who are introverted and reserved. We network with people in educational settings, churches, civic groups, and social/leisure contacts. Understanding how our Divine Assignments affect our relationships is the first step in sinking ourselves into the work God has given to us using who we know ourselves to be.

Your Divine Assignment is not based on your roles, but it will have a profound impact on how you view and handle your relationships. If your identity is centered in your roles and relationships, you are in danger of becoming unsteady in your self-concept as your roles change, which they inevitably do. From when you graduate from high school to when your own kids leave for college, and all kinds of role and relationship transitions in between, our relationships are changing in many ways. That's part of normal human development. The Call for All—love God, love yourself, love others—certainly doesn't change as your roles are adjusted; neither does your Divine Assignment. This is one of the remarkable benefits of knowing your primary God-given purpose.

Living your Divine Assignment will have profound implications for you. As you continue to see how it permeates your life, you'll see other people differently and make an impact on their lives, as well. The intimate partnership with God that it takes to pull off this transformation will revolutionize the way you see him and experience grace and abundance in your life. Evelyn sums it up well:

> Investing the time to uncover my personal mission statement set me free. I still to this day remember the weekend and that moment when so much became clear to me. It answered many questions... or should I say yearnings? It confirmed the desires of my heart. As I have moved forward in the past three years "living on purpose," I believe that I live more authentically now than ever. This not only impacts how I see myself but how I relate to others. I find myself encouraging anyone I encounter to uncover and live the mission and vision. I feel that I am more at peace and closer to the Lord.

It Starts with You

An absolutely breathtaking awareness is that God gave your Divine Assignment to you as a healing for you first, and then as a way to minister to others. Draw a set of concentric circles that resembles a target used in archery practice. Each circle represents a sphere of influence. The person you have the most influence over is yourself, so the center circle refers to you.

God knows what you need most to heal or experience in your life. As you obtain what you need from God, you become more aware of the true meaning of that quality. Then you can, in partnership with God, pass on to others what you've learned and experienced in an authentic and empathic way. For example, with my Divine Assignment to Stimulate Wisdom, I must first attend to the stimulation of wisdom in myself before I can fully share it with others. When someone finds their Central Passion to be Kindness, they must first embrace kindness for themselves before they can give kindness in its purest form to others. It's one way God keeps us honest and helps us not feel like fakes as we seek to truly live the particular call he has on each of our lives.

How can you give love if you don't really know what it is?

How can you help others find and claim their dignity if you haven't a clue about your own authentic dignity?

How can you stimulate compassion in others if you don't truly know what it means to be the grateful recipient of compassion yourself?

How can you introduce others to deep peace if you don't know how that impacts life firsthand?

I smiled in a mom's weekly group when Kristy quipped "I'm going to put barbed wire around my inner circle." To be truly transformed, you need to spend time getting a good handle on how your Divine Assignment applies to yourself first. Only then can you truly share the depth of God's call with others.

Your Divine Assignment will impact your life in profound ways. Libby, who discovered her Central Passion is Dignity, writes,

> When I realized that the concept of dignity rang true for me, it began to open my eyes in so many ways. As a child I had been treated in ways that

quickly eroded my dignity. There was nothing dig-
nified about being a receptacle of my father's hate.
Dignity is not a sense of arrogance or entitlement.
I am working toward a sense of dignity in the fact
that I survived.

Claudia, whose Divine Assignment is to Ignite Compassion, writes,

Personally, life has a more profound meaning for
me. Each task, project, or path that I choose to
embrace is a more perfect fit and is a joyous labor
not an overwhelming one. (That is not to say that
the carpooling and laundry don't overwhelm me....
They have little to do with compassion unless I
stretch the meaning to its limits!) However, I have
found that I am a balanced combination now of
energized and quiet. While I am far more at peace
with my own self and the direction I am headed
each morning, I am also, in that quiet state, more
energized for I know where my heart and head
are—together.

Who is next in your circle of influence? The second circle
is probably your spouse (if you're married) and your immediate family. Your closest friends might also be in this sphere.
The third circle might be general friends and the people
you're closest to at work. Your other colleagues may be
fourth, and your extended family could be fifth.

As you contemplate the people in your life, how will your
knowledge of your Divine Assignment impact them? For one
thing, you start seeing them in a clearer light. As Libby began
to see people through the lens of Dignity, she developed these
insights:

So many things in this imperfect world diminish
our dignity. God created us with a desire to be dig-
nified simply by being a creation of God. Human

choices eat away at this basic concept. As I interact with my family of choice, I am now more conscious of the verbal and nonverbal statements I make. My desire as a parent and as a spouse is that my family can have a sense of dignity no matter what the life circumstance. A garbage man, CEO of a Fortune 500 company, and a student can all feel a sense of dignity. They can all feel honor and pride with what they do and say each and every day. They can hold their heads high and soar with the strength of dignity.

As Claudia ponders what her Divine Assignment to Ignite Compassion has meant for her relationships with others, she says,

> I find that my relationships with people tend to be richer on two counts. First, through my journeys of compassion, I have met others who share the same concern. That is inspiring and creates a wonderful base for me in which to grow. Second, I feel that because I am at a new level of contentment, I have more patience for others who are not there, as well as a renewed level of dedication toward strengthening and nurturing my family and friends. I find that the days are more full of that which allows me to go to bed at night with a sense of pride, satisfaction, and contentment that even if small in scale I have made a difference in the life of someone or something that day.

The way you start to sink yourself into who you are and the work you've been given as it applies to the people you touch is profoundly powerful. In fact, it's the most lasting mark you will make with your particular purpose.

As you begin to piece together your two-word purpose, start trying it out specifically and consistently with the people around you. Part of your visioning, which you'll do in chapter

10, is to ask yourself, "As I'm living out my Divine Assignment, how will the people around me be affected? How will they be changed for the better? What kind of contribution will I make to them?"

A particularly exciting aspect of this part of living your Divine Assignment is that you might uncover some people in your life who you never knew needed you. These may be particular pockets of people you are now more excited about because you've gotten a clearer focus on what you're about. For example, my friend Libby went through this process and uncovered that her specific Divine Assignment is to Protect and Enhance Dignity. As she began to ask God what this meant for her life she thought about it for herself and her obvious circles of influence. But she also became more and more aware of a growing desire to be an advocate and provider for foster children. One of Libby's specific dreams is to assist foster kids who are transitioning out of the system into the "real" world by providing practical instruction on finances, household tasks, and career development issues, to name a few. She also wants to provide each foster child with a transition basket filled with lots of wonderful products and goods to make their first few weeks on their own more pleasant and less lonely. Life with the God who issues Divine Assignments is never dull.

Your Relationship with God

Knowing and living your Divine Assignment can have remarkable effects on your relationship with God. Living in lifelong relationship with God brings a closeness that keeps daily life in perspective. Jennifer, whose Divine Assignment is to Nurture Peace, says,

> The area of my life that has been affected the greatest is the quality of my time with God. True peace comes from a close personal relationship with God, and I am now more able to turn things

over to him and allow God to use me in whatever way he chooses. My relationship with God is richer, fuller, more trusting, and more dependent than ever before. I can't wait each day to see how he'll use me, communicating through the inner peace he gives.

Jennifer's growth underscores that the Call for All and discovering your Divine Assignment go hand in hand. When you are more able to receive and respond to God's love, your Divine Assignment becomes clearer. When you gain clarity in your Divine Assignment, you experience God's grace and peace in increasing amounts. It's a lovely circular relationship that just keeps getting better and better.

Gaining a sense of God's perspective in time and provision is also a powerful benefit in discovering your Divine Assignment. Claudia, whose Divine Assignment is to Ignite Compassion says,

> My relationship with God has perhaps grown the most. I finally feel at this stage of my life that I am truly walking with God. I have patience knowing that every prayer does not need to be answered immediately and that I don't need to be in control of my own destiny. What a relief! I feel that my days are in his hands and that if I am silent enough, quiet in my heart, and patient with his plan, I will be shown where my heart must go. Thus far, it has been a wonderful journey.

Kelly says having a sense of her Divine Assignment has made her more aware of God's minute-by-minute presence as she is constantly pleasantly surprised by the people and resources God plunks into her life to help her carry out her Divine Assignment. She feels God's care intimately as all she needs to do what he's asked her to do is provided faithfully and often humorously.

Perspective on the Past

Discovering our Divine Assignment can also put our past relationships into perspective. We may be able to say, "Oh that's why I interacted with that person the way I did." We might realize that something in his personality thoroughly challenged our Central Passion or blocked our Greatest Strength. John came to understand that his mother had completely undermined every ounce of his Central Passion of Courage he had as he was growing up. He was frustrated in his relationship with her because she made him feel afraid. He was frustrated with his father because his father never stood up to his mother. He just disappeared most of the time.

Now God rules and overrules, and it's entirely possible that in his interactions with his mother, John became more aware of his need for courage. It may not have surfaced as it did if she hadn't pushed him the way she did. Courage was a healing to him first, then something he could instill in others.

As you look into your past and look at relationships that have troubled you, you may find they were challenging to the very core of who you are and why you are here. Or, you might realize you clicked with a particular person because he had a similar Assignment or a complementary Assignment. By working together you could go further in your Divine Assignments than you could without them.

Discovering More About You

1. As you consider your Divine Assignment, why do you think it has been given to you as a healing for yourself first? As you consider how your particular purpose applies to you, what hopes and dreams is the Holy Spirit communicating to you?

2. What are your important relationships at this point? How will living your Divine Assignment alter them?

3. How will your particular purpose affect the relationships in your outer circles of influence? What will you hope for their lives as you come into contact with them and/or hold a position of influence with them? How will they be better people for having had your touch in their lives?

4. How does your Divine Assignment influence how you see other people in general?

5. What changes in relationships do you foresee for the future? What new relationships do you envision coming into your life? How do you think understanding your Divine Assignment will help you weather the inevitable changes in relationships we all encounter through life?

6. Ask God what he wants you to do with this new information. Write his answer.

ॐ

Gracious God,

Thank you for giving me a Divine Assignment to minister to my own unique life and circumstances. Thank you that you care so deeply about me as an individual that you have kept track of my life and all that has happened in and to me, and you have sent me a particular purpose that meets me right where I am. You are indeed a remarkable God.

Now that I have a sense of purpose, show me how you want to use me at this particular time in my particular location with the particular people who surround me. You have sent them to me and me to them for reasons I don't always see or know right off the bat. But I trust your plan. I know that all you want from me is to be myself and have confidence that you are working all toward good.

Help me to be faithful to my purpose. Help me to see and call forth your purpose in others so that together we may know and love you more deeply, have a keener appreciation for ourselves and each other, and change our world to more fully reveal your hopes and dreams.

In Christ's name, amen.

NINE

What's in Your Cupboard?

∽

*The strength and happiness of a man consists in finding out
the way in which God is going and going that way, too.*

HENRY WARD BEECHER

For several decades, Harry has been quietly going about his business at our church running an employment support group every Sunday morning, sometimes ministering to one person, sometimes several, always present. The irony of Harry is that you can't find out what Harry does for a living by asking him. He won't tell you. He has clever ways of skirting the question, but you'll never get a straight answer from him about his job. Harry's rationale? The answer to this question usually sounds like this: "I am a teacher" or "I am a plumber" or "I am a surgeon," and Harry doesn't want to be identified by a job title.

Harry knows that what we do does not define who we are. What we do expresses who we are. The difference is monumental.

I love to ask people this question: Was there ever a time in your life when you said to yourself, "This is that for which I was born"? Psychologists call these moments "peak experiences." They happen with regularity to people who are becoming self-actualized or are on their way to developing into all they were meant to be. Unfortunately, the psychologists claim it actually happens to only a few people such as Eleanor Roosevelt or Martin Luther King Jr.[1]

I think peak experiences happen to regular people with more frequency than we know. Peak experiences are the times when you feel you are living your Divine Assignment and using your favorite resources to fulfill it. Jody, a dynamic wife and mother writes, "I am fired up in the midst of a small group Bible-study format anywhere...anytime—especially in the midst of women, moms, and my peers. When I get the opportunity to bring the gospel message to mothers, I experience the power of the Holy Spirit!"

Rani, a beautiful and gifted psychologist and consultant from South Africa, describes her peak experiences: "I have those moments when I am standing and teaching about true leadership and purpose. On one of these occasions, I was teaching a group of corporate executives around a pool located in a beautiful mountain region. The setting was perfect and the group highly receptive. I felt this is what I was called to do. I realized that this did not feel like work at all—but play (with pay). I learned that I enjoyed being me."

Sara said she has these moments in life when she is encouraging and/or facilitating the growth of others.

Gerald said he knew he was doing something for which he was born "the first time I stepped into a classroom to teach. I felt this incredible sense of belonging and 'fit.' I learned that God gave me specific gifts to be used in teaching and exhorting others in his kingdom."

Marilyn is finding joy as she's settling more comfortably into the empty-nest stage. In this phase of her life, she's finding deep meaning in mission projects at her church that are "a match" for who she is and what she finds meaningful.

Michele finds peak moments in an organization of women who inspire her to live her Divine Assignment:

> It is not the organization itself for which I am born, but the sisters, for whom I am made. The relationship and the inspiration I have received and given to my sisters have made me a much better person. I have learned great compassion and humility from them. It is from their love that I gain strength to stimulate integrity both inside and outside the bonds of sisterhood.

A peak experience may surprise you and reveal something to you that you didn't know was inside. Catherine, whose Divine Assignment is to Create Hospitality, describes hers:

> Many years ago, a friend asked me if I would be interested in working with regional women's work for the church. I said yes. Little did I know she didn't want me to be on a committee, she wanted me to be the committee.
>
> I felt I wasn't ready. I hadn't been in the women's group that long, and I had never been an officer. All of a sudden I was advising 33 presidents of church women's groups on how they could improve their groups. It wasn't long before I found that my common sense and youth were my biggest assets. I was active in regional work for six years and even worked on the international level for several years as a volunteer. I was lucky to have someone see in me something that I didn't see in myself. I had never thought of myself as a leader up to that point. Now I know I am a leader.

What's happening in these peak experiences? Usually you are doing something you really enjoy doing, using a gift you may have known for a while you have, or possibly discovering one you didn't know about. Often you are engaged in an activity that has deep meaning for you, that answers the question: What do you feel is the world's deepest need? When you are struck with the notion that you were born for the moment you just lived through, your soul is confirming that you've just been in a situation that speaks to your Central Passion and your Greatest Strength and accesses interests, skills, talents, and gifts you find most pleasing to use.

Some of these experiences have to do with paid employment, some of them don't. But we can look at them and find out clues about where God wants us to be and when we are most aligned with our Divine Assignment. I firmly believe it can happen to more people in this world if only more of us become aware of the connection between living the Call for All, understanding our individual Divine Assignments, and applying the Divine Assignments to our relationships by using all of the gifts God has given us.

Your Appliance Garage

Getting a sense of what God wants us to do comes through the resources we have been given to carry out our Divine Assignments as our everyday lives unfold. To set the stage for this phase of exploration and transformation, I want to give you a visual image that we'll use throughout the rest of this book.

Imagine that your Divine Assignment is the electrical energy running through your house. This energy has one way to get from the internal circuitry to actually being used—the power outlet. But even the power outlet is not useful unless we *plug things into it* to make things happen. Now, we plug all sorts of things into these power outlets—hair dryers, televisions, lamps, coffee grinders—each of them carrying out the purpose of the electricity in various expressions of that electricity.

When we talk about "resources," we're diving into the realm of all the "appliances" we have at our disposal to manifest the source, the electricity. You will be amazed at the "appliances" you have in your garage. Some of them may be hidden way in the back of the cupboard or on the workbench right now. Some of them may not actually be the right tools for you. Some of them are appliances you use every day, and some will be more specialized. Some may become more important as your circumstances change. But we all have a wealth of appliances that we can hook into the endless energy resource of our Divine Assignments.

Let me give you several concrete examples of an appliance.

An appliance might be a skill. My husband, David, uses his abilities as a marriage and family therapist to express and bring life to his Central Passion of Wholeness. Because he believes so deeply in the need for each person to continually move toward wholeness, he uses his skills to make it happen. Wholeness is "what" he is here for, marriage and family therapy is "how" he makes it happen.

An appliance might be an interest. My friend Theresa has a deep interest in children. Her Divine Assignment is to Nurture Goodness. Theresa is happiest when she is interacting with children, helping them discover and apply goodness in their lives. Her interest in children is an outlet for her passion for Goodness.

An appliance could be a talent. My mother, Lenore, has a remarkable talent for entertaining. She loves to provide food, lay out a spread, decorate, and have all of the right things in place to make her guests feel welcomed and loved. My mother's Central Passion is Joy, and she plugs in her "appliance" of entertaining as an avenue to bring more joy to herself and others in her circle of influence.

An appliance may be a character trait. I am optimistic. It takes a lot to get me down. I always look for the health, growth, or postive outcome of a situation. My Divine Assignment is to Stimulate Wisdom. I use my character trait of optimism to keep me going as I seek to carry out my Divine Assignment on a regular basis.

Appliances are the gifts God has given us to do what we are called to do. Your talents, interests, skills, and character traits are all ways God has enabled you to sink yourself into the work he has given you to do while you're here on this earth.

A special trick is not to fall in love with the appliance while using it to express the source, and ultimately *the* Source. C.S. Lewis writes fictionally of an artist who was separated from God because he eventually fell in love with his paint instead of the Light that was the source of his passion for painting in the first place. Lewis, through the character of Spirit, cautions:

> Every poet and musician and artist, but for Grace, is drawn away from the love of the thing he tells, to love of the telling till, down in Deep Hell, they cannot be interested in God at all but only in what they say about Him. For it doesn't stop at being interested in paint, you know. They sink lower— become interested in their own personalities and then in nothing but their own reputations.[2]

Occupations, Jobs, and Careers

We spend our days in many different ways. Some of us have occupations which, for our conversation here, are pursuits, enterprises, or tasks that we carry out without pay. Occupations may be raising a family, raising money for charity as a volunteer, or keeping the household running smoothly. They are projects or roles that keep us occupied.

Some of us have jobs (which we may often be doing at the same time as we are carrying out occupations). A job is something we do for pay that isn't necessarily something we have a college degree for. We don't really intend to stay in the job for an extended length of time. It may be a position we hold between career moves to generate cash flow. A job may not hold personal meaning or a sense of real accomplishment or contribution. Paul, as a tentmaker, is an excellent example of what it may mean to have a "job." His passion was preaching and proclaiming Christ, yet he still had to put food on the table. He used a skill he had learned to make this happen, but I suspect he was preaching even as he was stitching.

Some of us have careers. Careers are the professions for which we studied or a paid position that we dearly love and are continually looking for ways to improve in to advance, to make a more complete and meaningful contribution. Careers feel more like a calling than a paycheck.

You could bet good money on the notion that most of us will have an occupation, a career, and a job at some point in our lives (sometimes all at the same time!). In chapter 12 we'll look at life interruptions that cause changes in employment status and necessitate all three for most of the population at one time or another. But for this chapter, we are going to look at the resources God has given that will steer us in the right direction of living our lives to the fullest, whether we find ourselves in an occupation, a job, or a career.

Quite often we get our resources confused with our Divine Assignments. We believe that the best God has for us as his hopes and aspirations is a certain job, or title, or achievement. The best God has for us is that we get to be fully who we are, fully using the resources he has given us that will bring us the most joy and bring about the greatest good. The more we can use our most beloved gifts and skills, coupled with a wonderful work environment, the happier we are, no doubt. But the career is never the assignment. The career is one "appliance" we have to express the energy generated by our Divine Assignments.

For example, my Divine Assignment is not to be a writer, but I'm a writer to help carry out my Divine Assignment, which is to Stimulate Wisdom. We'll be happiest and most helpful when we understand that we have been gifted with a set of interests, skills, talents, and character traits that uniquely equip us to enjoy our Divine Assignments as well as to effectively carry them out. Sometimes this will be on the job; sometimes it will be in community involvement. It is even manifested in the leisure or Sabbath periods of our lives.

The Nature of Our Gifts

Remember those words from the Central Passion list and the Greatest Strength list that didn't make the final cut, but that you had a difficult time letting go? It's now time to revisit those lists and pick up some of those words! We'll fit them into four categories—interests, skills, talents, and character traits—to get a big picture of your gifts.

Interests—Interests are activities, causes, hobbies, concerns, or passions that you have. They are things you like to do. They are places you like to go, people you like to help, ways you like to spend your money and your time. They can be something you do all by yourself, such as a hobby in the basement or something you do with lots of people, such as build a Habitat for Humanity house.

How can you tell what your interests are? Well, which section of the newspaper do you read first? What kind of magazines do you pick up in the grocery store? Look at your calendar and your checkbook. Where are your time and money going?

Skills—Skills are things you have learned to do along life's way—perhaps on jobs or through some kind of specialized training. A skill may be typing, organizing, decorating, making spreadsheets, or teaching. You may enjoy the skills you have or you may have acquired them just to get along in your work. You may actually be really good at something you do but not enjoy it. For example, when I worked in a large, suburban church, I had to develop the skill of administration. Part of my job was to oversee finances, program calendars, and people resources. People would say to me, "You are so good at administration." I would smile and thank them and say to myself, "And I hate it." Nonetheless, our skills are an important part of who we are. They are elements to be considered as we "sink ourselves into" who we are and the work we've been given.

Talents—While skills are acquired, talents are natural abilities we have been born with. They can be artistic, physical, academic, or interpersonal in nature. They are aptitudes you can remember having for as long as you can remember! They may be sharpened with practice, education, and use, but they're still capacities we have always had. They may find their expressions in skills we learn as we grow, such as an artist learning various techniques or a doctor learning various treatments. Talents seem to be endowments from birth simply waiting to find manifestation as we grow, explore, and mature.

Character traits—What are the words people would use to describe you if your name came up in a meeting or at a party? They are words like punctual, thorough, funny, aggressive, thoughtful, or easygoing. These are character traits. If you look back to the personality continuums you did in chapter 3, you'll begin to get a feel for the wide array of words that can be used to describe you. As you are looking at this category, make a list that encompasses the traits you think others see in you. Make another list that embodies the qualities you see in yourself. How often do these two lists intersect?

Now how do we make a careful assessment of these gifts to ascertain how we can sink ourselves into the work we've been given to do? Spend some time in introspection, in listening prayer for the lovely voice of the Holy Spirit, who can be counted on to meet us in questions such as this when our hearts are open. Self-assessment and reflection on who we have been in the past and who we believe ourselves to be in the present can give us terrific clues as to how God would have us invest our lives in the carrying out of our Divine Assignments.

We can simply take notice of times in the day, week, or month when we are at peace and feeling "in the groove." As we take note of what makes us happy, we can echo one way my friend Sara gets hints on the resources she's to use to carry out her Divine Assignment: "The things that come easily for me are clues about how God has equipped me." Her understanding of God's call on her life is reminiscent of the 1981 film *Chariots of Fire*. Olympian Eric Liddell, in response to his sister's chastisement that he should be working as a missionary, replied, "God made me fast, and when I run I feel his pleasure." Where do you feel God's pleasure?

Another evaluation tool is to elicit feedback from others regarding our skills, talents, and gifts. The trick is to ask for this feedback from people whom we trust and who have no self-serving agenda for us. For example, if I ask my boss about what I'm good at, and that boss doesn't want to tell me what he sees as my true gifts because he is afraid I'll leave my position with his organization, that boss cannot be trusted to give me accurate information. Hopefully there are other people who have your best interests at heart who can give you positive feedback

As you identify these interests, skills, talents, and character traits, you may recognize that not all of them feel right for you. Some of them are interests you picked up because people close to you significantly influenced you to be interested in what they are interested in. You may have gotten good at something you actually don't like to do. You may become aware that a particular character trait is something you bought into along the way to fit in, but it's not really who you feel you are. Or you may become conscious that gifts you have long left dormant are actually the very tools you need and want to use as you seek to carry out your Divine Assignment with joy and passion.

It's time do to some sorting.

What to Keep, What to Toss

Life is a constant process of deciding what we need to keep and what we need to toss. Sometimes this involves loving and incisive analysis of things we have thought or believed simply because we were taught a certain way. Jesus took many and varied opportunities to make this point to the people of his time, oftentimes making the point in front of those who opposed him with a crowd looking on.

> Another time he went into the synagogue, and a man with a shriveled hand was there. Some of [the Pharisees] were looking for a reason to accuse Jesus, so they watched him closely to see if he would heal him on the Sabbath. Jesus said to the man with the shriveled hand, "Stand up in front of everyone."
>
> Then Jesus asked them, "Which is lawful on the Sabbath: to do good or to do evil, to save life or to kill?" But they remained silent.
>
> He looked around at them in anger and, deeply distressed at their stubborn hearts, said to the man, "Stretch out your hand." He stretched it out, and his hand was completely restored (Mark 3:1-5).

It was time for the Pharisees, for this man, and for all the people gathered around Jesus to know that the old way of doing things was being called into a new order—the order of love and grace. Jesus showed this man that, yes indeed, it was all about him. Jesus restored him and his dignity and treated him like a human being instead of an object under the law.

A new kingdom way of looking at things is encapsulated in one of Jesus' interesting phrases in his earthly ministry: "You have heard that it was said...but I tell you..." (Matthew 5:27,38,43). Just because something "has always been done this way" doesn't mean it's the way to do it now. God's specialty is continuous revelation, renewal, and transformation.

This type of cleaning and sorting applies to our ever-growing awareness of who we are in relationship to God's hopes and aspirations for us. Did you ever wonder what God hopes and aspires for you on a regular day-to-day basis? We can know this as we do some honest sorting.

Closet Cleaning

About every six months I tear through the closets, cup-boards, basement, and garage in our house, muttering under my breath that I'm sick of the clutter, and we're not going to have stuff just hanging around that is keeping me from feeling free, effective, and efficient. That's the week our garbage pile is extra big, and there's a carload of bags and boxes that go to Goodwill. While my first motive is to get my house in order, a secondary blessing is realizing how much good I can actually do when I don't keep things in my life that could benefit others much more. I feel better when the trash is gone and when the bags and boxes have been donated to others who might be looking for the jeans my kids have out-grown and the sweater that may have been an impulse pur-chase and isn't being worn at all.

I have three options: keep, throw away, and give away. Everything is sorted into one of those options.

When I'm cleaning a closet, I go through the clothing sec-tion by section, or in categories. I sort through the tops, the bottoms, and the dresses. We'll go through three categories as we decide what to keep, what to throw away, and what to give away as we sort through the interests, skills, talents, and passions you have. The categories are motives, the opinion of others, and generational influence. They are all cleverly inter-laced, yet distinct in the power of their influence.

Motives

God is so funny. Oftentimes, just when I'm getting ready to write on a subject, I'm presented with a situation which, if I live through it, will be an excellent example of what *not* to do in the point I'm trying to make. Sigh. Such was the case the autumn I was putting this book together.

I was presented with an opportunity to co-chair a bazaar with a delightful woman from my church. The proceeds were to benefit the choir in which my daughter sings. They were raising money to go on a trip to Carnegie Hall to sing. Very cool woman, very cool cause, very cool people I would hang out with while we were putting this event together.

The only trouble is, I really didn't run it through my Divine Assignment, and I honestly didn't consult the Holy Spirit before I said yes. I made up all kinds of reasons in my head as to why I should do this and, frankly, most of them were self-serving.

So I got into the process and became more and more irritated with the phone calls I needed to make, the communication I had to have with people, and the preparations I needed to be involved with to bring this event together. Fortunately, my co-chair was a remarkable woman and an organizational wizard.

Long story made short, my motives for being involved were crummy so my alignment with God was off. I was out of sync with God's specific hopes and aspirations for me personally, and that made me a cranky, sad person.

Volunteering is not the only category that is affected by faulty motives. We can have out-of-whack reasons for staying in a certain career or relationship. We can have goofy objectives for wearing what we wear, eating what we eat, and living in the house we live in. Everything we do has a motive.

Motives are defined as a need or desire that causes a person to act. My very favorite way to think about motives is the image I get when I think of how I've heard hunters trap monkeys in the wild. I don't know if it's true or not, but it's a great illustration! Trappers bait a trap with a banana. The trap is a box that has wooden slats around the sides, spaced perfectly apart so a monkey can stick his unclenched hand through, yet can't pull his hand clenched around a banana back through. Pretty clever little trap. If the monkey wants to keep the banana, he has to keep his clenched hand in the box and be snared by the trappers. If the monkey wants to be free, he needs to drop the banana and run away.

The point is this: Whenever you have grabbed onto a tempting little morsel only to find out it has turned into a time-robbing, energy-sucking, peace-stealing black hole in your life—drop it! Drop it as quickly as possible, and head a different direction.

How do our motives form? Our wants and needs that cause us to act can take shape when we are very young. In fact, many of them do. We want to be loved, and we need to feel secure. We take cues from important others around us as to what will bring us the love and security we crave. We decide to shape our behavior in ways that will maximize mental and emotional comfort and minimize discomfort.

The closet-cleaning process is extremely helpful in weeding through our mental and emotional needs that make us do the things we do. The trick is that we need to know ourselves and be ruthlessly honest about why we do what we do. This is where the clear eye that Jesus spoke of is so helpful.

> The eye is the lamp of the body. If your eyes are good, your whole body will be full of light. But if your eyes are bad, your whole body will be full of darkness. If then the light within you is darkness, how great is that darkness! (Matthew 6:22-23).

We need to have clear eyes as we see ourselves so true light can shine on who we are and what our motives seem to be. We need to have clear eyes to look out on God's world and make good choices about what we invest our lives in and why.

Many times our motives are closely tied to the second category of sorting, the opinion of others.

The Opinion of Others

The older I've gotten, the more fond I've grown of this thought: What others think of me is none of my business. Yet all of us continually walk a fine line between caring what others think and not caring what others think. We have to be discerning about who to listen to and when. There is a time to listen to others and a time not to. Neil Simon said,

> I firmly believe that if you follow a path that inter-
> ests you, not to the exclusion of love, sensitivity,
> and cooperation with others, but with the strength
> of conviction that you can move others by your own
> efforts, and do not make success or failure a criteria
> by which you live, the chances are you'll be a
> person worthy of your own respect.[3]

One of the toughest career decisions I ever made was to say no to two people whom I deeply respect and whose opinion I greatly cherish.

They made me an offer that I was finding hard to refuse, not because of the position they were offering me, but because of those who were making the offer. They were offering me a position that would fit very well with interests I had expressed, gifts I had exhibited, and character traits that were in keeping with interacting with and nurturing women. I knew I had the interests, gifts, and character traits, but I wasn't convinced about the actual setting. And not because the setting had anything wrong with it! There was just something inside that told me not to take this position, that there was something else to do with all I had and was going to have.

And it was precisely the lack of concrete "evidence" that made saying no even harder. While the people involved were very gracious in accepting my refusal, I suspected they were secretly scratching their heads at my decision.

What was coming on the horizon was the birth of several books and the subsequent speaking, leading, and consulting that would come from them. But none of us knew this with scientific certainty. We were all walking by faith, not by sight.

That's what we're called to do sometimes in putting aside the good opinion of others. We are called to be faithful to the quiet promptings of the Holy Spirit. We are called to put aside what seems like the obvious choice to do something that we might not yet know in a concrete way. We are called to look a little foolish and perhaps not very savvy in putting aside a great opportunity. We are called to risk the disfavor of people we deeply respect and whose opinion and influence mean a great deal to us.

Ted Geisel was one of my favorite modern-day philosophers. He was most commonly known by his pen name, Dr. Seuss. I have found his viewpoint in the following quote to be very thought-provoking and certainly a great closet cleaner: "Be who you are and say what you feel because those who mind don't matter and those who matter don't mind."

So as you look at your interests, which ones are you hanging onto to maintain the good opinion of others? Are there skills you keep using even though you don't enjoy using them because you get accolades or recognition from others? How about talents? Is there a talent you know you have that you won't let out of the box because you aren't sure how other people will respond? Is there a talent hidden away because you are afraid in using it you won't be as good as others who have a similar talent? And what of character traits? Do you persist in showing various character traits even though they really don't reflect who you truly want or believe yourself to be? In all of these areas, new kingdom thinking, the kind that says, "It's time to look at all of this in a new way—God's way" is the key to making the healthiest, most joy-producing decisions.

Generational Influence

Maybe you had a Great-grandma Sophie. My father's grandmother was named Sophie Sobko. She was straight from the Ukrainian homeland. She brought my grandmother over "on the boat" when my grandmother was three. Sophie was an old-world great-grandmother if there ever was one.

I start remembering her vividly when I think back to when I was about 12. By then Sophie had almost no teeth, bosoms that went to her waist, and she laughed with a merriment that was a cross between a wheeze, a guffaw, and a cackle. Her house always smelled of cooked cabbage, and she waddled when she walked. She was great.

Great-grandma Sophie came to know the Lord later in life, but once he took hold, she was alive with loving him. Whenever we would visit her, she and I would wind up sitting on the big, overstuffed sofa with her sitting on my left. She would tell me great stories. And always, somewhere in the midst of the conversation, she would lay her right hand on my left knee and say in her awkward English, "I pray God power on your life." I thought that was kind of cool, and I felt it sure couldn't hurt.

It wasn't until later in life that I really began to understand that my Great-grandma Sophie was giving me a gift. Some people would call it positive prophecy; some would call it a blessing. Whatever you call it, it had a dynamic influence on me when I realized what my Sophie had done for me. She had bestowed on me a living memory. It was a memory of her that, through the Holy Spirit, turned into an everyday invocation for me to understand that God was with me and for me at all times.

I hope you had a Great-grandma Sophie—someone who passed along loving assurances that you were unique, worthwhile, and needed on this earth. She didn't tell me what I should be, just ensured that I would be happy and blessed along the way.

History, on the other hand, is absolutely littered with the broken lives of people who pursued a particular passion, career, or lifestyle simply because their families wanted them to. Maybe you've done this a little bit yourself.

Or maybe you've followed a certain path because your father never got to go down that path himself. Perhaps he wanted to be a teacher, but because of family responsibilities or parental expectations, the opportunity was out of geographical, emotional, or financial reach. Our lives are full of, as Carl Jung put it, "the unlived lives of our parents." To start to tease apart the strands of these powerful unlived lives, I suggest a simple exercise. Get out a pad of paper and write down all the things you believe you should do, have, and be in your life. When you get to the end of the list, go back over it and put a name beside each item indicating who it is who wants you to do, have, or be that (and who might have wanted to do that themselves but never had the chance). Turn to the next blank sheet and write out your list with only the items on it that had your name beside them. I call this the generational grocery list. Keep writing out your list until you are absolutely certain you have only the things on your list that truly belong to you.

Or maybe you were discouraged from following a particular dream because of your gender. One of my clients told me of an evening meal with her parents when she was in junior high school. She had just discovered what a psychiatrist was, and she was very enthusiastic about looking into it as a career. At dinner she bubbled over with her newfound career possibility. Her father slammed his hands on the dinner table, rattling china and silver and announced, "That's the stupidest thing I've ever heard. Women do *not* become doctors." She was crushed, and that was the end of that discussion. The mark it left on her was not only that she couldn't be a doctor, but she was limited simply because she was female. The reverse can happen when a young man wants to be a dancer or artist. Not a typically manly profession, his parents might try to steer him into something more "gender appropriate."

Maybe you've followed a particular course because your mother was really good and successful in that arena, and either you believe you will be too or there is family pressure to carry on the business.

Perhaps you've gone through a course of study because you thought it would make your grandmother happy or because your grandfather was paying the tuition and you needed to follow his wishes in order to keep the funds flowing.

Now, this is a *very* important piece of the generation influence assessment, so listen carefully. As you are making this assessment, you are *not* going about the task of disrespecting your family of origin or those who came before them. This is not condemnation, it is information. You are gathering insights that will help you decide what interests, skills, talents, and character traits you want to move ahead with and which ones are now to be put in the toss and give-away bags. As you go through this process, you may uncover issues that will elicit anger, remorse, pain, or grief in you. Those emotions, believe it or not, are gifts from God steering you toward what's truly yours to keep and what you need to toss or give away. Do not hesitate to get some good, short-term counseling to help you put these memories and issues in proper and healthy perspective.

Not Job Counseling

I am not in the business of job counseling, so I'm not going to give you advice on how to use your passions to find the right job for you. The truth is, as we'll see especially in chapter 12, we can't always find the perfect job.

What we can come to understand in this segment of the discovery is that we can be God's partner no matter where we are. Whether you are in an occupation, a job, or a career, or any combination of the three, you can live your Divine Assignment. Now, the more of your resources you can use throughout your life, the happier and probably more effective you will be. But always be open to the fact that your resources may be used in ways that are surprising to you. As you become clearer about who you are and stay close to God expecting the unexpected, the more you will find ways to live your Divine Assignment wherever you are using as many of your resources as you can. God will not gift you and then leave you without opportunities to use the gifts!

Theresa is a perfect example. Several years ago she was in a group of mothers who went through the five-week Divine Assignment series designed just for moms. In our time together, she realized that her Divine Assignment is to Nurture Goodness. She could see how that applied to herself, her family, and her friends. Yet she had another longing in her heart that she could identify as working with children, but she didn't know what that meant.

For several years she went about her daily business, tending to her very active family and sticking close to God. She was living her Divine Assignment in all she did. But she still had the "longing."

Just this past year at our church, my husband, who is the director of a counseling center, began a new program called New Day for Children of Divorce. It's a much-needed ministry for kids of all ages, from very little through adolescence, to come and be with trained and caring people who meet with them every other week. This program gives these kids a safe and understanding place to explore the range of emotions common to children going through this emotional transition.

Theresa is a child of divorce. God loves Theresa and wants her to live her Divine Assignment to the fullest. And God had to work a few other things out (like my husband finishing his doctoral dissertation on children of divorce) before the opportunity could come to the surface for Theresa to live more fully her Divine Assignment, using more of her resources. Whenever I see Theresa and ask her how New Day is going, her eyes brim with tears over her compassion for her "kids." She speaks of how grateful she is that she can introduce them to the goodness of themselves, their lives, and other people who care about them, and, most importantly, the goodness of God's love.

As I talked to Theresa about telling her story in this book, she hastened to remind me that God is still at work to bring things into even clearer focus. In the next few years, her own children will be in school. Theresa feels that God is walking with her and working with her even now to bring the ways they are going to minister together into even sharper focus. She's still discovering appliances—personal resources, gifts, and talents—she didn't know she had or that have been dormant for years. Her last word on the subject was "patience."

So look back over your interests, skills, talents, and character traits. Pretend you are sorting through your closet of resources and you have three options: keep them because you really like them and find them fun, valuable, and useful; give them away because it's not something you can use anymore but someone else might like; or throw them away altogether because it's something that is honestly trash.

Discovering More About You

1. Make a list of your ten favorite interests as defined by causes, activities, hobbies, and passions. Remember to revisit the words you considered for your Central Passion.

2. Make a list of ten skills you possess.

3. Make a list of ten talents you have.

4. Make a list of ten character traits you recognize in yourself.

5. As part of your closet cleaning, look at what motives you hold for keeping various skills, talents, traits, or interests. Remembering that motives are defined as a need or desire that makes a person act, what were your motives for the past six things you have said yes to in

your life? Did they stem from what you deeply believe to be important or were they influenced by outside forces (even the forces of the past)?

6. The second category for closet cleaning is the opinions of others. Whose opinions are important to you? Where do their opinions actually help you be a better, more complete, more authentic person? Where do their opinions hinder your genuine self-expression, cause you to doubt your resources, or make you feel poorly about yourself? Who's in control of the influence the opinions of others has over you?

7. The third task in closet cleaning is to consider your generational influences. How have people in the past influenced you? How have these been positive influences? How have these been negative influences? What do you want to carry forward? What do you want to leave behind?

8. As you think about your resources as appliances, what appliances have been given to you that you feel are genuinely helpful and fun for you to use as you express your Divine Assignment? What appliances have been given to you that you would now rather return to the store, give to Goodwill, or quietly place in the trash?

9. Ask God what he wants you to keep and what he wants you to let go of. Write his response.

❦

*A*lmighty and gifting God,

Thank you for the clarity that comes from going through these exercises. With clarity comes energy and a sense that I really can make a contribution to this world in your name. Not only that, I can enjoy who I am and what I do.

Help me to continually discern between what I authentically need to keep in life and what isn't useful and helpful to me as I seek to serve you and others with my Divine Assignment. Help me make peace with what others want from me and what is honestly mine to do. Help me find deep joy in being aligned with you.

Thank you for showing me what's possible, and that your kingdom can indeed come on earth as it is in heaven.

In Christ's name, amen.

TEN

The Power of
Partnering with God

❧

A vision without a task is but a dream,
a task without a vision is drudgery;
a vision and a task is the hope of the world.

AN INSCRIPTION ON AN OLD ENGLISH CHURCH

One of the most potent setbacks people have in their continuing transformation—the part of the transformation where the Divine Assignment is actually given heart, hands, and feet—is that they can't tell the difference between a dream and a vision.

Two examples of a dream came up in two different groups I worked with to help the individuals discover their Divine Assignments. One gentleman, a student development administrator at a local university, said his dream was to be a major league baseball player. Now in his forties and never having been on any kind of team except Little League and school sports teams, it wasn't likely that he would fulfill this dream. His age, his nonoutstanding baseball skills when he was younger, and his current family situation made it look rather doubtful that this was going to happen.

A woman who was a line supervisor in a factory told her group that her dream was to be a fighter pilot. Again, for reasons of age, skills, and family situation, it was unlikely she would realize her dream.

As my friend Catherine said, "Just as a maple tree will never be a Christmas tree, I know there are things I can never do."

Dreams without the corresponding skills and opportunities, either that we make happen or come to us through the course of life, are fun to think about. They're clues about what we find interesting, and they even highlight qualities we may want to exhibit in what we're currently doing. But dreams are not really visions unless we have the gifts and graces to carry them out. I dreamed of being Miss America when I was a child, but…well, that's a whole 'nother story!

Dreams are often about possessions, personal achievements, or the kinds of things James was talking about when he said, "When you ask, you do not receive, because you ask with wrong motives, that you may spend what you get on your pleasures" (James 4:3). Dreams can be the product of the bumper sticker we mentioned earlier: "It's all about me."

Michael Keaton played a musician/father/husband named Jack Frost in the movie *Jack Frost* (1998). One evening, after having missed his son's hockey game that he had promised to attend because of having a very exciting and successful recording session in the studio with his band, Jack apologizes and talks to his son about dreams. He tells his son that he had always dreamed of being a musician, of being a musician who was really good and could make a great living at what he did. He recognized that his son may have dreams of being a great hockey player. But, he cautions, you have to be careful because sometimes dreams can make you…then he struggles for the words. His sweet son, in a noncondemning yet truthful few words says, "A selfish jerk?"

Dreams can also make us feel sad, remorseful, or frustrated when what we see doesn't match reality.

Visions, on the other hand, are given by a very exciting God—a God who wouldn't call us to something that we were not going to be graced to do, even if we know we don't have the gifts and graces to carry out the vision at this time. A vision, even though it may seem out of reach, is attainable when we account for the powerful partnership that we have with God. Even though the vision doesn't match reality, it still makes our hearts beat faster because we know in our deepest parts that it's possible.

A vision is something that God lays on your heart. The more closely aligned you are with God's heart and his hopes and visions for you, the more deeply you feel it for yourself and the more passionately you want to see the vision come true.

Yet the single biggest hesitation I encounter in people who I help through this growth process comes when it's time to articulate a vision about what their lives and the lives of others will look like as they start to actively live their Divine Assignments. Because writing a vision is a scary thing, people stop at this point in the process. The result is similar to James' understanding that faith without works is dead (James 2:17). Recognizing a Divine Assignment without understanding how to carry it out makes for a dissatisfied soul. God's ability to live out his hopes and visions for you and with you is halted. Now that you know who you are, it's time to figure out what you're supposed to do!

The vision-writing process is so absolutely critical to the faithful living of our assignments that God spoke specifically of it to the prophet Habakkuk:

> And then GOD answered: "Write this.
> Write what you see.
> Write it out in big block letters
>   so that it can be read on the run.
> This vision-message is a witness
>   pointing to what's coming.
> It aches for the coming—it can hardly wait!

And it doesn't lie.
If it seems slow in coming, wait.
It's on its way. It will come right on time"
(Habakkuk 2:2-3 msg).

Why is vision-writing so daunting? I have found four reasons why people shy away from this critical element of discovering their Divine Assignments. They are quite legitimate concerns and have good resolutions when we view life from God's perspective.

It's All About Stuff

The first hesitation is that, in our heart of hearts, we are put off by people whose visions we have heard that are focused on what they are going to achieve or the lifestyle they are going to attain. Many popular vision-writing exercises have participants focus on the kind of house they're going to live in when their dreams come true, what kind of clothes they're going to wear, what kind of car they will drive, and what kind of vacations they will take. While these are indeed fun things to ponder on occasion, the discerning heart knows that at the end of the day, none of us is actually very inspired by visions of personal gain or accomplishment. In the end, we admire people—and our own visions—for making this world a better place. As long as we're encouraged to envision all that will make us materially happy and comfortable, we will be stunted in being able to articulate the hopes and visions God has for us. God isn't as impressed with what we're going to accomplish as he is with what we're going to contribute.

The Longest Leg of the Journey

The second obstruction people face is the inability to see the road at about the midpoint of the journey. Oddly enough, they may express what they envision for the short term, especially in how they believe their Divine Assignments will impact their lives and the lives of those around them even in the next six months. We're also able to convey what we see in the very long term, much as if we were writing the script for our eightieth birthday party toast. But it's in the middle part, between 6 months and 50 years from now, that people feel stymied. We are hesitant to think and speak in these terms for one major reason: What if it doesn't happen? Boy, wouldn't we be foolish then!

This is actually one of the most luscious ways God displays his partnership with us. God calls us to articulate the "what" as we see it forming in our hearts. The two questions that leave us feeling uneasy about saying what we see are "how" and "when." But remember in chapter 5 I said your Divine Assignment is a partnership? You and God each have a role in the partnership. You do your job of letting God plant the "what" in you, then you let God do his job of bringing about the "when" and the "how."

In the Discovering More About You section of this chapter, I will walk with you through three time frames for vision writing. Even though the middle time seems the most daunting, don't let yourself off the hook. It's in the middle where we do most of our living. You deserve to have a clearer picture of what kinds of appliances (resources) God wants you to plug in to the power source of your Divine Assignment and what the output might look like.

Living with Limits

Oddly enough, the third obstacle that many people run into is the concept of limits. We don't want to be tied down, and we think that by expressing what we feel in our hearts, we're then committed to doing what we've written down. We don't like boundaries, limits, anyone or anything (even a statement we ourselves have written) telling us what to do. Or, on the other hand, we're wary of having visions that seem limitless, taking us way beyond our comfort zones or mental/emotional/spiritual limits. This is a downside of the bumper sticker thinking, when we focus on visions and carrying out visions as being all about us.

Psalm 121 uses an intriguing word when describing our relationship with God. Verses 7 and 8 say: "The LORD will keep you from all harm—he will watch over your life; the LORD will watch over your coming and going both now and forevermore." The Lord keeps you. That means you are free to explore all kinds of limits in his gracious providence, but you will always know when you have bumped up against your boundaries. Those limits may prove to be something you tried to take on that you are honestly not interested in or equipped for. Those limits may be natural spiritual limits of ethics, kindness, relevancy, or decency. Either way, the spiritually discerning know when they have reached a limit. In walking closely with God, we can envision remarkable things that stretch us and our faith. The limits are often much broader, deeper, and higher than we expected.

At the same time, if God's limits for you seem to be far broader, deeper, or higher than you anticipated, you can be comforted in knowing that, yes indeed, you are limited. But we are called not by our gifts but by the grace Christ has given to each of us (Ephesians 4:7). We are limited; God is immeasurable. If we ground our vision writing in God's "incomparably great power" (Ephesians 1:19), then we can trust that we're not just writing visions for ourselves that we have to carry out ourselves. Our visions rely on the infinite abundance of God and our God-given resources working in concert to bring about what God wants most to see happen in us and in the world.

A finite human being partnered with an almighty and infinite God. Strange coupling, I know. And it's even more strange that the idea came from God himself. That's grace.

Who in the world really wants to be unlimited? Who in the world really wants to be limited? In understanding and articulating the vision God, your partner, is giving you, it will be the right scope for the two of you to tackle. We will always be mindful that we are talking about our limitations combined with God's limitlessness or abundance. When you are completely sated in living the revelation—the true revelation—you will be so completely amazed at how one thing leads to the next. The string of opportunities you have available to you will just keep spinning off the spool. You will not be bored.

The Split Screen

A fourth barrier to vision-writing is the belief that what you are currently living is not part of the vision. We get a funny little notion in our heads that the vision has to be something pretty different from what life is right now. Indeed, for many of us, when we start the process of discovering our Divine Assignments, we do so because our spirits are restless and a bit (okay, maybe more than a bit) dissatisfied with how life is going. But as the Assignment becomes clearer and we start to sink ourselves into who we are and the work we've been given, we may find that we are already fulfilling some of the pieces.

In this sense, it's very healthy in vision-writing to ask, "What's working in my life at this time that I want to keep?" In other words, what parts of your vision might already be true and be up and running? You want to build on those strengths. At the end of the chapter, I'll ask you to think of several pairs of words and consider what kinds of things fit into each category. You'll get a better sense of what's already a part of your working vision and how your vision is leading you to an even more God-ordained, God-aligned life.

Imagine you're watching a split-screen television. One side of the screen represents the vision. The other side of the screen is your everyday reality. One function of the vision is to bring the desired into better focus so we can concentrate on that side of the screen, eventually enabling it to become the entire screen. Some of the elements of the desired screen may be happening in your everyday life already and will continue to be pictures you see on the screen.

The Principle of Unfolding Miracles

One of my greatest simple pleasures in life is the collection of Page-a-Day calendars I keep around my house. You know the ones I mean? You can get cartoons, diet tips, house-cleaning reminders, and inspiration near the phone, as you brush your teeth, when you boot up the computer, and while you're eating breakfast. Each day is something new in little bite-sized morsels meant to nourish you through the day.

I happen to have a Thomas Kinkade Page-a-Day calendar by the kitchen sink. I love his artistry. He's as much a master of the artistic word as he is the paintbrush. It's from Mr. Kinkade that I learned about "the principle of the unfolding miracle." He says, "You can learn to trust the principle of unfolding miracles—and in the unfolding miracle that is your life. Trusting the principle of unfolding miracles sets you free from the need to have all the answers." Participating with God in articulating and writing your vision is simply a tool to help you more fully live in the reality of unfolding miracles. Writing your vision is like getting a Triptick from AAA, helping you know which direction to steer the car. Writing the vision helps you know that your Divine Assignment is to go to Winnipeg, Canada, not Montgomery, Alabama. But writing the vision should never be mistaken for an unwavering travel document that will never change or have a few surprises in it.

I am the happy illustration of this very principle of unfolding miracles.

When I started seriously writing my vision statement, there was never any mention whatsoever about teaching at a college. The thought didn't even enter my mind. I didn't want to do it, I simply had no inkling of it for my life.

One August morning my friend Mary, who works as the adjunct faculty coordinator for the community campuses of our state-wide community college, called. An instructor had to back out at the last minute from teaching two sections of public speaking, and it was one week away from the start of fall term. She was in a bind.

A mutual friend had very kindly suggested Mary talk to me, and Wham! I became a college instructor. Funny thing is, over the course of my time with the college, we discovered I was actually better equipped to teach psychology and sociology. So now I teach a full course load of classes to some of the most amazing students Indiana has to offer—and I love it! I drive away from my classrooms feeling like the luckiest woman alive to get to do something I love to pieces and to be able to make a contribution to the lives of others.

But it wasn't in the original or subsequent versions of my vision statement. I never once wrote it down. Except...

As I was musing to my husband one day about my utter satisfaction in teaching and the fact that I had never "seen" it for any of my vision statements, he said, "That's not true, Rob. You've always loved helping college students, especially the new ones who need lots of support and guidance. You, in your heart of hearts, have always wanted to do this. Remember how you felt about your experiences at Taylor?"

And he was completely right. While I was an undergraduate at Taylor University, I was deeply immersed in student services as a peer mentor to freshmen. I loved it and had harbored in my heart the hope that one day I would be in student development. But I missed the educational boat in terms of getting the graduate degrees I needed to make that happen professionally.

Yet in the unfolding miracle of my life, God took care of it another way.

My point is this: Have fun in the vision-writing phase of discovering your Divine Assignment. There so much energy that comes from opening your heart to the possibilities of God's hopes and plans for you. God, I believe, delights in showing us glimpses of the road to help set us in the right direction. I also believe God loves to reserve the right to surprise and unfold his miracles along the way for us. The entire process of living your Divine Assignment is one of partnership with God where God is in the lead. Being open to receiving the vision, articulating what you "see," stepping out in faith, and staying loose in the saddle for God to unfold miracles in your life keeps the stage set and your heart prepared to truly experience a life marked by a deep and growing relationship with "him who is able to do immeasurably more than all we ask or imagine, according to his power that is at work within us" (Ephesians 3:20).

So Write the Plain Vision

In the Discovering More About You section of this chapter, I'll take you through three time frames of vision-writing, giving you prompts for each time frame. Don't be afraid or daunted. You write your vision as God's partner. Write your vision in pencil, if it makes you feel better! Write your vision as your own. It's not someone else's desire for you; it's your own articulation of what you see. It doesn't have to be complicated at all, just descriptive and a picture that you can honestly see for yourself. As you are writing your vision, make use of the three following guidelines.

1. Let the words flow without an internal critique constantly stopping you with nagging questions, such as, "You really don't think that can happen, do you?" or "How in the world do you think you'll finance this?" or "What will the neighbors think?" This critic should be noted but not heeded, and should certainly not stop your writing.

2. Use all of your senses as you write the vision. This is called "vivid visioning" and helps your brain connect your present to your future. We tend to think in pictures, and as we more clearly describe the pictures with their sights, sounds, tastes, smell, textures, and movement, we accomplish two things. The first is that we will recognize the vision when it unfolds. We'll be able to inwardly smile at God and say, "I knew that was going to happen." You can't imagine how connected to God you feel when that happens until you've

experienced it. Second, it helps us cut away all that isn't in the vision so we can stay focused and on track.

3. Write your vision as journal entries. In other words, date the top of the page as the day you are writing about in the future, then descriptively tell what happened that day using the present tense.

I had an interesting experience regarding the power of writing entries as the present. It actually puts you in that time. As I was learning to vision-write, I was sitting outside a building on a lovely San Diego evening. It was about five o'clock and the sun was lowering on the horizon. I was completely engrossed in writing a future journal entry about a morning when I was up just before my family, and then how the morning progressed as they woke up and we all helped each other get ready to meet the various tasks of the day. There I sat writing and writing about seven o'clock on a future morning when a lovely woman passed by. She said hello to me. I smiled at her as I looked up from my writing and said, "Good morning." I get a big kick out of the time I "lived" in a different time frame simply through the power of visioning.

My friend and fellow traveler Evelyn gave me a gift when she clearly articulated what writing her vision has meant to her:

> It has helped me remember the big picture and not give up. Especially in the 2½ years right after I discovered my mission and vision. I was in the process of making some career changes so that I could live my mission more fully. Having a mission statement helped me stay focused. One thing I did that helped tremendously was find a tangible reminder of my vision. For me it was a bottle of Vermont maple syrup. It was something that I wrote about in my vision during a retreat. In part of my vision I write about having breakfast in the morning with my husband. The menu included

harvest grain-and-nut pancakes with warm maple syrup. One of the ladies in my group suggested that it not just be warm maple syrup, but Vermont maple syrup. I took her suggestion. About a month later this same lady sent me a bottle of Vermont maple syrup. I was touched. I decided to use it as a reminder of my mission and vision. I kept that on my desk for the entire 2½ years that I was transitioning from corporate America to my vision of becoming a life coach and trainer. There were many days when it seemed like I would never live my vision. It was those moments when I would look at the bottle and think, "You will get there. Remember the vision. Remember the big picture."

God wasn't kidding when he told Habakkuk to write the vision, keep it before him, and then be patient. Visions take time to unfold. Timing is everything, as my mother always told me. But having a clear sense of the future self calling to the present self with confirmations and affirmations that you're headed in the right direction can help you stay focused, help you get through times when the going seems a little slow, and help you be patient. Nancy, the mother of two small kids and a woman with considerable financial skills and interests, shared this very moving update on where she is right now in her life after having discerned her Divine Assignment. It's very moving because Nancy is so honest about the unfolding nature of what it means to live in God's hopes and visions for us:

I was walking on the beach last Thanksgiving (over a year ago) and thinking about my Divine Assignment—I think I was considering what a typical day would be like in the future. I got really excited as I realized that I think part of living out my Divine Assignment involves helping people get out of debt. Specifically, lower-income individuals who often are strapped with medical debt because they don't have insurance. I envisioned starting a non-profit where

I would give them the tools to get rid of that debt—who to call, what to say, etc. Not to do it for them, but to teach them how to do it themselves. I don't know when it will happen, but two "funny" things happened not long after that.

First, I got a call out of the blue from an individual who sits with me on the Habitat family selection committee (the committee that interviews and qualifies applicants for a home). He, like I, was bothered by all the medical debt we see from these applicants and wanted to start a fund to assist them in some way! And he wondered if I had any thoughts about how to go about doing that!

Second, I met a man from our church whose wife was on the pastoral nominating committee with my husband. This gentleman owns a medical debt collection agency. So I asked him whether he had any thoughts on this concept. Turns out, he has a lot of thoughts. We went to lunch and discussed the idea at length. I got some great input.

Coincidence? I think not! Bottom line, not too much more has happened in the past few months. But I do keep it in my mind, and although I feel like this isn't the right time for me, I think someday it will be.

I am so deeply respectful of Nancy because part of this not being the right time is her sensitivity to the intertwining of outer and inner forces that will let her know when the time is right. She is not forcing something to happen. She is tending to other important things in her life right now. The two encounters she tells of are confirmation that she's moving in the right direction. She has the vision. It's becoming more plain, and, though it seems to be taking a while to become reality, she is holding on to it—all as God instructed.

Write the vision. Make it plain. It may take some time, but wait for it. It will not linger past its due time.

Discovering More About You

1. What is the difference between having a dream and having a vision? What dreams have you had? What visions have you had?

2. Why is it important to write the vision and make it plain? How does an emerging vision keep us on track and help us feel more fulfilled?

3. The first time frame for vision writing is six months. By looking at pairs of words, you can better define where you are. For instance, in your life at this time, what is abundant and what is scarce? What is healthy and what is sick? What is peaceful and what is chaotic? What is working and what is broken? What are you enjoying and what are you not enjoying?

4. The second time frame is 6 months to about 80 years old. This is a large amount of time for most of us. So break your vision into manageable time frames.

   Early Adulthood (20 to 40 years old)—Will you be single or married? What about kids? If yes, when and how many? What's happening with your social network and extended family? Do you have an occupation, a job, a career, or a mix of all three? Where are you living? What are your community involvements? What's happening with your finances and your health? How do you spend your free time? How is your Divine Assignment coupled with the Call for All playing out in each of these life arenas? Write a complete and detailed description of a weekday and another description of a weekend day.

Middle Adulthood (40 to 60 years old)—Are you single or married? If married, what is your relationship like with your spouse? What's happening with your kids, if you have any? Are you facing some transitions, such as career changes, children growing and moving out of the house, health considerations, and role reversals as you become more of a caretaker for your aging parents? What is your vision regarding transitions and how you manage them? Where are you living? What are your community involvements? What is meaningful to you as a volunteer? What's happening with your finances and your health? How do you spend your Sabbath time? How is your Divine Assignment coupled with the Call for All manifesting and informing what you are and do in this middle adulthood time of your life? Write a complete and detailed description of a weekday and another description of a weekend day.

Early Older Adulthood (60 to 75 years old)—Are you married or single? Are there children and grandchildren? What are they doing and what is your relationship like with them? Are you still working in your career? What are you doing, with your discretionary time? What interests and causes have captured your attention? What is your social network like? What is happening with your finances and your health? How do you stay connected to other people? What are you giving, and what are you receiving? How do you spend your Sabbath time? How is your Divine Assignment coupled with the Call for All lived out through your everyday life? Write a complete and detailed description of a weekday and write a description of a weekend day.

Now, it's not that I don't expect you to live past 75 years old. The fact is many of us are going to live well beyond that. But you get the idea and could write a wonderful time-frame description for every 5 years after 75, if you wanted to!

The business administrator at a church in Indianapolis gave a full-day Divine Assignment seminar to her support staff as a perk for the wonderful work they did all year. As Susan was going through this phase of the Divine Assignment discovery, she remarked, "It's like writing your future autobiography." There is great power in writing such an autobiography. It clarifies what you believe to be important. It's like your future self calling to your current self saying, "Here's some of the map to help you find me along the way!" It gives you a better connection to the distinctiveness that God intends for you as you live your Call for All *and* your Divine Assignment.

5. The third time frame you'll write about is a retrospective eightieth birthday toast. Write a journal page describing what people say about you as they celebrate with you at your big party on your eightieth. You can write this from your own perspective or as your best friend, child, or spouse. Include in your detailed narrative what you want to have said about the following aspects of your life: health, spiritual, social, career, family, community involvement, friends, financial. For what do you want to be remembered? What would they say about how you lived each aspect of the Call for All? What would they say about how you lived your Divine Assignment?

What you want said about you on your eightieth birthday starts today—right this minute. The choices and responses you make in life every minute have an impact on what life will be like for you when you're 80 and beyond. To be able to articulate what you want to be remembered for is part of God's way of telling you what you need to be doing right now to be on an aligned track with his hopes and visions for you.

6. Are you more comfortable with the thought of having limits or of being limitless? What do you believe to be God's perspective on limits? Why do we need them? Where do they hold us back? What do you think is the most healthy stance regarding living with limits?

7. What are some of the unfolding miracles you've seen in your own life or in the lives of those you love? Are you open to unfolding miracles or is everything pretty much planned out in your mind about how your life is going to go? How might the principle of unfolding miracles be a comfort to you?

8. Ask God what part of the vision he's most excited about for you at this point in time. Write his response.

❧

Gracious and vision-giving God,

Throughout spiritual history you have graced your children with visions of the world you and they can together create. Thank you for the honor and delight of being one such child. Help me have fun writing the vision, knowing that my life will always be a delicious mixture of things you reveal to me in advance and surprises you hold along the way. Help me to bear graciously all I "see," understanding that you are ultimately the reason I live.

Thank you for the relationships and resources I have been able to ponder and see incorporated into my future. Help me to continually cut away what isn't truly part of your hopes and aspirations for me. Help me to anticipate in faith.

In Christ's name, amen.

ELEVEN

Who's Winning Your Mind Games?

✧

If a man does not keep pace with his companions, perhaps it is because he hears a different drummer. Let him step to the music which he hears, however measured or far away.

HENRY DAVID THOREAU

*P*aul says to his Galatian friends, "Each of you must take responsibility for doing the creative best you can with your own life" (Galatians 6:5 MSG). You and I are artists. Whether you feel creative or not, you are the artist of your life in God. But it should come as no surprise that from time to time we will face artist blocks. I call these "Purpose Poppers." They are internal states or mind-sets that cause us to feel that the flow of our Divine Assignment has been dammed to a dribble. They are the mind games we play with ourselves that can stop us in our tracks.

But God never leaves us with a paintbrush in hand and nothing to paint. So there are "Popper Stoppers," or ways of thinking, believing, and interacting with God that help us get past, through, over, under, or around the blocks that come our way on the journey. These Popper Stoppers help us get on with the business of doing the creative best we can with our lives.

Paul's Purpose Poppers

Paul articulates two very specific Purpose Poppers: thinking more of ourselves than we ought and comparing ourselves to others. These are actually two facets of the same Purpose Popper—self-absorption.

When we think of ourselves more than we ought, we are teetering on the precarious edge of self-sufficiency. We believe we can do everything. We have it all handled. We can take on anything that comes our way. This Purpose Popper eventually ruins our ability to carry out our Divine Assignment. Our Divine Assignment is *always* a partnership with God, and if we're not in that dynamic alignment we wear out, become disillusioned, and begin to think we heard the call incorrectly.

Comparing ourselves to others can lead to self-doubt or an unsavory sort of self-satisfaction. Comparing ourselves to others always has a dual-headed, double-trouble focus. We've either got our eyes on ourselves or we have our eyes on someone else. Those are the only two targets our eyes can see when we're in comparison mode. The problem with this is obvious: We no longer have our eyes on Christ, "the author and perfecter of our faith" (Hebrews 12:2).

In either case, self-satisfaction or comparing ourselves to others, we can't even cover the first three bases of the Call for All—love God, love ourselves, love others—let alone have enough sense to discover our authentic and unique Divine Assignments.

So the Popper Stopper for self-absorption is to put our sights on God. The reason we focus on God is not initially to get back on track, although that will be a wonderful side benefit of the real blessing. We center on God because it feels good. Recognizing once again God's trustworthiness and faithfulness in his love for us is very relaxing and freeing. We can breathe again. We get our eyes back on God by appreciating his creation, by spending quality face-to-face time with him, by employing a mind-set used by the psalmists when they were distracted:

Praise the LORD, O my soul;
    all my inmost being, praise his holy name.
Praise the LORD, O my soul,
    and forget not all his benefits—
who forgives all your sins
    and heals all your diseases,
who redeems your life from the pit
    and crowns you with love and compassion,
who satisfies your desires with good things
    so that your youth is renewed like the eagle's
(Psalm 103:1-5).

What About the "P" Word?

When the past and all of its little minions start creeping around in your head, taunting you and giggling about your failures, your poor decisions, your thoughtless words and deeds, you can indeed suffer from the Purpose Popper of unworthiness.

This little Purpose Popper is the one that sniggles at you from the basement, telling you that you have not lived a life worthy of the calling you have received (Ephesians 4:1). This insidious liar will tell you that no one with a past like yours could possibly be fit to receive the love God has for you, to love yourself, to play well with others, and to have a uniquely designed Divine Assignment God laid out just for you.

This big lie of unworthiness frequently haunts people who have been abused. It is estimated that 40 million persons living in the United States alone have been sexually abused. That doesn't count the people who have suffered physical, emotional, mental, and spiritual abuse. And it doesn't include the many people who have never told someone what they suffered. A potent weapon abusers use against the people they abuse is to convince the victims that somehow the abuse is their fault. If they hadn't acted the way they did, said what they said, looked like they looked, or been at a particular place at a particular time, the perpetrator would never have abused them. This extremely powerful lie keeps millions of people from living a life of freedom, health, and purpose. It makes the victims believe they are not worthwhile people and that they should be continually punished for what happened to them.

The first way unworthiness pops purpose is to persuade the victim that he doesn't deserve a Divine Assignment. Through the conditioning of abuse, the abuser convinces the abused that he doesn't deserve anything at all, least of all a significant reason for being. People who feel unworthy in this respect carry the burden of feeling that God could never look on them with the favor he regards others with. Other people are loved enough to deserve all the best God has to offer. Other people are the apple of God's eye and the beneficiaries of his hopes and aspirations for them. But not the one who considers himself unworthy of even the most basic of God's consideration.

The second way unworthiness pops purpose is assuring the victim that he is inadequate to the task of carrying out the Divine Assignment. The one who is feeling unworthy in this regard decides that he may indeed have been given a Divine Assignment, but he doesn't have what it takes to live up to the Assignment. He may even have proved himself to be right from time to time through self-fulfilling prophecy, so eventually he just gives up.

Perhaps your sense of unworthiness doesn't come from the kind of serious and blatant abuse we've been talking about, but it came from consistent and persistent little voices of the past telling you that you don't count, that you're not good enough, that you can never measure up. Basically these people are telling you that Jesus didn't die for you. And that's not true!

Whatever the lie of the past, God's Popper Stopper is new life—new life that comes every morning, every moment, certainly every time we become aware of the fact that we want it afresh for ourselves.

> Now we look inside, and what we see is that anyone
> united with the Messiah gets a fresh start, is created
> new. The old life is gone; a new life burgeons! Look
> at it! All this comes from the God who settled the
> relationship between us and him, and then called
> us to settle our relationships with each other. God
> put the world square with himself through the Mes-
> siah, giving the world a fresh start by offering for-
> giveness of sins....Become friends with God; he's
> already a friend with you (2 Corinthians 5:17-20
> MSG).

There is only one Popper Stopper for the ghosts of the
past, and that is to continually set your sights on completing
the circle of friendship that God has already extended to you.
Friendships take time and energy. They take reciprocal ded-
ication and devotion. God's brilliance in this kind of strategy
is clear. If you are focused on your ever-deepening friendship
with God, you don't have time to focus on much else. Every
time your past pops your sense of purpose and worth, take it
to Jesus. Sit down with him and talk it over. What does he say
to you about it? You may also want to sit down with a well-
trained, wise, and compassionate professional who can help
you see the lie for what it is. God has the power and the love
to clear your past and set you on the path he hopes and
aspires for you.

When God Can't Get Through

A variety of mind-sets and heart-sets can actually hinder
God's ability to communicate with us and give us the love
and direction we need to carry out our Divine Assignments.
We'll look at three of them: unforgiveness, ingratitude, and
fret.

Unforgiveness is a deeply potent Purpose Popper. Very few
times does Jesus indicate God won't do something healing or
restorative, but in Matthew 6:15, Jesus said if we don't forgive

others, God won't forgive us. Is that because God hasn't for-given us? Is that because God's actions are dependent on our actions? No! God forgave everyone everything as Jesus died. God set us free from the nagging fears of unforgiveness. God can and does forgive us before we even know we need it. What Jesus was saying is that if our hearts are hardened with an unforgiving spirit, we let God's loving forgiveness bounce off.

Unforgiveness does indeed toughen our hearts not only to being forgiven ourselves, but to many other gifts of grace that God offers. When we are unforgiving, we don't allow God to fully embrace us, much like a squirming, resistant child putting up a barrier for a loving parent who wants to hold him. Since our own unique identity is such an influential gift from God on our sense of who we are, if we are squirming and fighting God through an unforgiving spirit, we are impeding God's ability to fully reveal his hopes and visions for us.

Ingratitude keeps us from the blessing of knowing and understanding God's gracious direction for us. We deny God's very essence when we are not grateful. God, in all of his abun-dance and cleverness, can't get through to us because we don't even understand who he truly is. When we do under-stand, we tap into the truth of one of my very favorite lines in all of Christian music: "Praise God from whom all blessings flow." To understand that God's blessings flow gets us back into the healthy, truthful perspective we need to have to be hooked into God's design for us.

> Gratitude may be the ultimate vocation for Chris-tians. We engage in whatever mission the Lord has given us not because we must, but because we may. People who are thankful for all the grace they have received want more than anything to give gifts.
>
> If we are grateful, we cannot help but live our lives as a witness to God's salvation. If we are not grateful, no matter how hard we try, we can never have a Christian vocation. That's because Christians

discover their mission only as a response to being in love with the grace of God.[1]

An ungrateful heart isn't necessarily a hardened heart, just an unenlightened heart. Ingratitude may not necessarily be defiance, just indifference. Either way, God can't get through.

Fret is a Purpose Popper of the first degree. Psalm 37, whose central and most beloved verse is "delight yourself in the LORD and he will give you the desires of your heart" (verse 4), refers twice to fretting as a lifestyle or mind-set that separates us from the kind of delight in the Lord that will hook us up directly with the desires of our hearts. When we are trusting, we know that what we need will turn up when we need it. We know we don't have to have all the answers or resources in sight. We know that God makes our paths firm when we stay focused. When we address this Purpose Popper, we use the Popper Stopper of understanding that we may not always know "how" or "when," but we do know "who" and "why," so we are safe.

There are many "offensive ways" lurking in all of us, and forgiveness, ingratitude, and fret are certainly top contenders as the most common. The psalmist, too, must have felt the sting of a clouded heart. He must have known the pain of seeking God's face only to find that his own heart was in the way. Let's join him in his prayer, using the Popper Stoppers of forgiveness, gratitude, and faith to clear the way for God to make our way clearer:

> Search me, O God, and know my heart;
>   test me and know my anxious thoughts.
> See if there is any offensive way in me,
>   And lead me in the way everlasting
>   (Psalm 139:23-24).

A Divided Heart

When you ask God to reveal his Divine Assignment for you, be assured he will. Discovering your Divine Assignment is one of the wisest things you can do in this life, and when it comes to wisdom, James assures us:

> If any of you is lacking in wisdom, ask God, who gives to all generously and ungrudgingly, and it will be given you. But ask in faith, never doubting, for the one who doubts is like a wave of the sea, driven and tossed by the wind; for the doubter, being double-minded and unstable in every way, must not expect to receive anything from the Lord (James 1:5-8 NRSV).

Along with the wisdom to know and understand our Divine Assignments, we will probably also need wisdom to know and understand what needs to be weeded out of our lives. If we don't exercise this weeding process, we are in real and serious danger of being double-minded and unstable because of our divided hearts.

As Christians, we can experience a divided heart in three ways. The first way is to be serving two gods who are not compatible with each other. Jesus must have known that we have a tendency to do this because he made a pointed statement to his followers on the subject:

> No one can serve two masters. Either he will hate the one and love the other, or he will be devoted to the one and despise the other. You cannot serve God and Money (Matthew 6:24).

The second way to have a divided heart is to be constantly second guessing our own motives in a way that isn't healthy or productive. "Is this really what God wants, or is it just something that I want?" Well, what if it's both? Wouldn't that be great to serve a God who was so brilliant and loving as to mesh the desires of our hearts with the hopes and aspirations he has for us? Intending to please God and seeking his will pleases God.

And last, we may have divided hearts because we are trying to focus on too many things at once. I recently heard a great description that hit home with me at a particularly vulnerable time. Many of us are paying attention to and trying to do one-eighth of eight things instead of 100 percent of one thing. We may honestly be well-intentioned, thinking we can handle so many things at once. And often these things are inherently worthwhile and good, but when there are too many of them on our plate, we become spiritually overweight and sluggish from too much too often. It makes me think, with a smile, of Paul's assurance that God would never give us more than we can handle. I smile because I know that is true; I just have to ask myself about all the things I've heaped upon myself that God never intended for me to do!

An Irresistible Force

If we see a particular way in which our Divine Assignment can be used, perhaps in a relationship, we get excited. We feel it's a call on our lives. We see the opportunity and want to go for it. Yet if the outcome isn't what we hoped, we might try to force ourselves on the person, the job, or the committee. This is the Purpose Popper of impatience.

Claudia wisely understood what it meant to live a lifetime under the guidance of her Divine Assignment when she said, "My Divine Assignment helps me relax because I know I have the rest of my life to Ignite Compassion." The Popper Stopper for impatience is perspective—the perspective of knowing that time is always on our side when living the Call for All and our particular purpose because God is in control.

Jesus, who certainly had an excellent command of his Divine Assignment, knew that there is only one approach to take to really be sure we're where we want to be and that what we are offering will be authentically helpful:

> Here I am! I stand at the door and knock. If anyone
> hears my voice and opens the door, I will come in

and eat with him, and he with me (Revelation 3:20).

If the one with the most compelling Divine Assignment of all is willing to wait and not force himself on anyone, any situation, or any opportunity, we can certainly be patient, as well.

Dry Well

One of the most interesting Purpose Poppers I have ever heard came from a very bright and delightful client I had the pleasure of working with on an individual basis. As she articulated what kept her from realizing and living her Divine Assignment, I recognized myself in her words. It's the Purpose Popper of limited resources.

Clare was an artist. A very talented artist. She worked with paints, textiles, and embellishments. The works she brought into my office for me to look at were absolutely breathtaking. But she was at a standstill, unable to feel some of what she needed to understand in the Call for All. She was feeling her particular purpose in her creativity had been dammed to a trickle.

She did what everyone needs to do when they are in a dry time—she was ruthlessly honest about her thoughts and feelings, trying to purify her heart to see God more clearly. I completely respected what she was doing because sometimes when we voice what's bugging us, it seems so unreal as we say it out loud. But keeping silent only makes it worse.

This beautiful artist told me of a powerful worldview her parents, who endured and survived the Great Depression, had passed on to her. Even though her circumstances were so different, the mind-set was still deeply embedded. Clare told me whenever it was time to eat or to use some sort of resource, her parents would caution, "Just remember, when that's gone, there isn't any more." As she said those words out loud and applied them to her own creative blockage, she realized she was hoarding her supplies, indeed her very talent and ideas, for fear that when they were gone there wouldn't be any more. Once she got the Purpose Popper out in the open, she could start to heal and apply the reality of Paul's assurance: "And God is able to make all grace abound to you, so that in all things at all times, having all that you need, you will abound in every good work" (2 Corinthians 9:8). She made a huge leap forward in her understanding of what God was transforming her into as she then made little transformations day by day, trusting God's provision.

I understood Clare very well. As a writer, I often psyche myself into an unproductive funk as I look at the pages and pages I still need to write for a book with the trepidation that I am going to run out of words before I fulfill the expectations of my contract. In those times I enjoy being reminded of the widow Elisha encountered in 2 Kings 4:1-7:

> The wife of a man from the company of the prophets cried out to Elisha, "Your servant my husband is dead, and you know that he revered the LORD. But now his creditor is coming to take my two boys as his slaves." Elisha replied to her, "How can I help you? Tell me, what do you have in your house?" "Your servant has nothing there at all," she said, "except a little oil." Elisha said, "Go around and ask all your neighbors for empty jars. Don't ask for just a few. Then go inside and shut the door behind you and your sons. Pour oil into all the jars, and as each is filled, put it to one side."
>
> She left him and afterward shut the door behind her and her sons. They brought the jars to her and she kept pouring. When all the jars were full, she said to her son, "Bring me another one." But he replied, "There is not a jar left." Then the oil stopped flowing. She went and told the man of God, and he said, "Go, sell the oil and pay your debts. You and your sons can live on what is left."

Clare's oil is paint and fabric. My oil is words. What's your oil, and how can God show you that you will always have enough for what you need—and often much more left over?

Wanting Things to Be Just Right

The Purpose Popper of perfectionism manifests itself in many ways. They all have to do with faulty thinking. We'll Popper Stop four of them.

The first kind of faulty thinking is called "all or nothing" thinking. Either you are going to be perfect at living out your Divine Assignment or you're not going to do it at all. A sure-fire Purpose Popper is not wanting to move ahead with your Divine Assignment until you sense that things are perfectly in order. Or you may feel that somehow you are out of alignment with your Assignment if things don't feel as smooth or as rosy as you thought they would be when you initially heard the voice telling you "this is the way, walk in it."

Some artists want to wait for perfect conditions to live out their Assignments. Writers want perfect quiet. Painters and photographers want perfect lighting. Surgeons want perfectly sterile environments. Parents want the perfect amount of time and money to be "good" parents. But conditions are so rarely perfect.

"All or nothing" thinking leaves you stuck because things are never perfectly in order for you to live your Divine Assignment. Those who do it best know they often live their Divine Assignments best when things aren't perfect.

A second kind of perfectionistic faulty thinking is "catastrophizing." We tell ourselves, "I better not try because I might fail, and that would be awful." We hesitate to tell others what we know we're about because they may catch us in a moment when we aren't living our Assignments well. When we catastrophize a situation like that, we believe that it would be just terrible if that happened. We think we would irreparably ruin our reputation, and worse, others would be telling everyone else about our failure. The problem with this thinking is not in the concern that we may falter, because those of us who are realists know that's bound to happen. The hitch in the thinking is when we make a mountain out of a molehill and let our minds race around thinking of all the terrible things that could come about because someone discovered our failure.

A third type of faulty thinking that barricades our ability to discover or live our Divine Assignments is "overgeneralization." You probably have fallen flat a time or two as you tried to let God love you, or let you love yourself, or let yourself love others. This Purpose Popper is the thought that because you have failed once, you will always fail.

A fourth type of faulty thinking is "emotional reasoning." This Purpose Popper is a double whammy of degrading emotions coupled with a downward cognitive spiral. These thoughts tell us, "I *feel* like I haven't done a very good job at living my Divine Assignment, so I haven't done a very good job at living my Divine Assignment." Because we may be having a bad day or week or month and our emotions are in a depressed state, we may let the negative emotion take the place of reasonable evidence that suggests something different.

All of these faulty thoughts are marked by one central theme—the fear of failure.

A story is told about a famous pub in Europe. It was a beautiful, quaint little pub until one day a stein of ale was spilled onto one of the walls. The stain was unsightly, and the owner was more than a little distressed over the mess and what he knew would be needed for a cleanup and restoration of the wall.

One of the patrons of the pub happened to be a local artist. With his art supplies in hand and a vision in his heart for what could happen with the impossible stain on the wall, he set to work to transform the gross imperfection into something beautiful.

All night he worked. The next day when the pub opened for customers, they were treated to and delighted by a breathtaking masterpiece, the center of which, barely now distinguishable as such, was the formerly wretched mess.

Impossible, messy, wretched mistakes can be transformed through an artist's vision and an artist's touch.

"What if I fail?" The question is not "What if?" it's "When?" Everyone fails at some time or another, even in the transformation process. And when you do, what does it really mean? What is failure in your eyes anyway? Remember we each make our own definition of success grounded in the first three elements of the Call for All—love God, love ourselves, love others. What if you fail? Will God love you less? Doubtful. Will you love you less? Maybe—and that's something you'll have to work on and come to terms with. Will you be impeded from playing nicely with others? Only if you allow yourself to be. Any failure can turn on a dime when you allow God to love you, love yourself as God loves you, and seek to be a good and decent person to those around you.

And don't forget the possibility that you may be afraid to succeed! Perhaps Maya Angelou was right when she suggested that we are actually intimidated by our own magnificence. Be it failure or magnificence that we fear—the fear needs to be faced and addressed.

Creativity cannot coexist with fear. Creativity knows it's free to make mistakes. Creativity is linked to inspiration, or literally living "in spirit." Creativity uses imagination, resourcefulness, and originality that can only be born of a mind that is healthy, curious, uninhibited, and liberated. Paul told his friend Timothy, "God doesn't want us to be shy with his gifts, but bold and loving and sensible" (2 Timothy 1:7 MSG). So we need to do whatever we need to do to make our minds and hearts healthy and grounded. Our hearts and minds will be strong and bold when we remember that we are perfectly loved because "there is no room in love for fear. Well-formed love banishes fear" (1 John 4:18 MSG). And there we are, right back to the beginning. Remember the first Call for All? To receive and respond to God's love.

Discovering More About You

1. Have you compared yourself to others? How is this counterproductive to loving yourself? How does it interfere with your ability to receive and act on your Divine Assignment?

2. What are some of your favorite ways to set your sights on God? What do you like to do to get your mind and heart refocused when you have gotten out of whack? What might you experiment with just for fun?

3. What in your past hinders you from feeling worthy or capable of the Call for All and your particular Divine Assignment?

4. If you were to sit down with Jesus to talk over what is bothering you about your past, what do you think he would say?

5. Of the three Purpose Popper heart-sets that hinder God from getting through (unforgiveness, ingratitude, and worry), which one are you most susceptible to? How do you get back on track?

6. Are you trying to tend to one-eighth of eight things, instead of giving full focus to one? Even if you decided to tend to one-fourth of four things, how would that change your life right now? Understanding that God

will never give us more than we can handle, what might be some things you have taken on under your own will?

7. Have you ever tried to force something to happen? What was it, and how did it turn out? What insights did the experience give you about yourself and about God?

8. The widow in 2 Kings had as her only resource a jar of oil. She seemed to have more problems than resources. What's your "oil," and how can God show you that you will always have enough for what you need—and often much more left over?

9. Have you ever let yourself engage in any of the faulty thinking of perfectionism? Knowing that the root of perfectionism is the fear of failure, how can you reframe failure or get a more realistic definition of what it means to fail? It's really healing to take a look at God's perspective on our failure, as well. What do you think he would say to you?

10. As you look over the Purpose Poppers and Popper Stoppers, what do you sense the Holy Spirit is trying to tell you? Write his response.

❧

Loving and gracious God,
Your Divine Assignment for me must have remarkable potential to change me and to change my world because there sure are a lot of ideas and notions in my head to keep me from carrying it out. Knowing that I'm in the middle of a war between what you hope and

aspire for me and the other side that seeks to keep me down and unproductive, I acknowledge to you that Purpose Poppers I carry around need to go!

You are so generous, God, to provide a Popper Stopper for each of the thoughts and heart-sets I can conjure up that keep me from you. Help me to know and understand your Word better, to tuck it away in my heart and will so that I cannot be separated from you and your designs for what I am to be and to do.

In Christ's name, amen.

TWELVE

Life Interruptions or When the Deer Smacks Your Car

❧

When we can't pursue our passions,
we must put passion in our pursuits.

THOMAS KINKADE

They honestly seemed to have come out of nowhere. They blended so well with the winter-colored cornfield that we didn't see them coming, even in broad daylight. The first three missed us pretty cleanly, for we had come to a stop realizing in a split second what was happening. The fourth barely missed us. The fifth, well, we're not quite sure what was going on with the fifth, but the smallest and last of the thundering herd of deer smacked directly into the passenger's side of my nearly new car. The deer hit the car, flipped up into the air, did a somersault, and landed on its back in the ditch on the other side of the road. Amazingly, it hopped up and ran away to catch up with its friends. Our trip had just been interrupted in a very abrupt, unmistakable event. As I pointed out to the insurance agent, we did not hit a deer—a deer hit us.

Life interruptions occur all the time. Emergency heart surgery, a divorce, finding out a daughter had an abortion, a sudden drop in the stock market—life has lots of interesting unpredictabilities. Some of them are mild; some are horrific. All of them necessitate we look at life in a different way, which can include our own reevaluation of identity.

It's Different Than I Thought It Would Be

There's no getting around it. Life is unpredictable. The faster our culture goes, the faster the changes come. Health, relationships, and careers seem to have minds of their own and leave many of us thinking, *This was not part of the vision I had for myself. I'm not going to be able to live my purpose under these conditions.*

In his book *When God Interrupts,* Craig Barnes, pastor of the National Presbyterian Church in Washington, D.C., makes this observation:

> I have yet to meet an adult who is living the life he or she planned. Some are thrilled about that: "Thank God life turned out so much better than I had hoped." Seldom does a week go by, though, that I don't meet as a pastor with those who are a long way from thanking God for a loss of what was cherished. Nobody wants to be abandoned.[1]

Indeed, one of the most intriguing aspects of this Divine Assignment concept is that people equate their Divine Assignments with the circumstances of their lives, and then they are left wondering what in the world they're supposed to do when they experience a loss, a reversal, a setback, or the ever-creeping realization that things aren't actually going to turn out as they had planned.

I am deeply indebted to the many people who, as I shared the unfolding of this process with them, wistfully commented that they wonder how they are going to live out their purpose in the context of their terminally ill parent or child, their financial situation that doesn't leave much room for chasing an entrepreneurial dream, or their own perceived disability that seems to block them from realizing the dreams they have in their hearts or the expectations they have for themselves. These are the people who are the closest to realizing the most remarkable part of this whole spiritual process—our purpose is not about our relationships, our finances, our career, or our health. Our purpose is lived in spite of these outward circumstances. We are never without our Divine Assignments.

Walking with God is often less about fairy tale-like conditions and more like slogging it out like a normal person on an everyday basis.

When Life Gets in the Way

Holding back tears, mounting the stage in front of hundreds of townspeople, family members, and former students, Glenn Holland took the conductor's baton from Gertrude Lang's hand after her deeply moving speech. This final scene from the remarkable film *Mr. Holland's Opus* (1995) highlights the reality that we often believe we were sent to earth to do one thing, only to find, as we look back and survey, that we were given a much larger purpose. Glenn Holland believed as a young man that he was to write music. Life circumstances such as having a child, discovering this child had a significant impairment, and just keeping up with the responsibilities of being an adult necessitated he take a teaching job that kept him from the one thing he primarily wanted to do—write music. In the end, however, Ms. Lang, whom he had significantly impacted, pointed out in a speech honoring his 30 years of teaching that he had indeed written a significant piece of music—music on the hearts of everyone he had touched and changed for the better in those years.

Have you ever had an expectation of something you were going to do only to have someone significant in your life become ill or incapacitated? Has a financial reversal blindsided you and kept you from fully living your career or a meaningful role? Have you ever gotten to be an age when you thought things would be one way and they were actually another? It's tempting at those points to feel like we're not living our purpose. The powerful reality is that we can live our Divine Assignments no matter what situations we're in, no matter how blocked we feel we are in achieving something. Our ability to live our particular purpose is never interrupted, although we may not get to use all of our resources as fully as we would like.

The Waiting Game

Is the time right to be fully active in your Divine Assignment? Or do you feel like a servant of God in waiting, watching his hand for the next specific directive because you're not sure where to go from here? I asked my friend Michele when she has felt blocked from contributing all she wants to contribute in her world. She said:

> That would be now. We had a great sermon today about waiting for Christmas, and when we were young we think that when we become adults we do not need to wait. The irony is that the older we get, the more we have to wait. We wait for our driver's license; we wait for graduation. We wait to meet someone special. We wait to have children. We wait until they are gone. We wait to find the right job, then we wait to retire from it. The list goes on.

There are five members in Michele's immediate family. When there are five people in your family (or even two), you may feel like you have a clear vision of what you want life to be like, but it just takes some time for values and mind-sets of the others to work out so everyone can be on a similar track. You're all in the same book, just not on the same page. So as Michele is waiting for the circumstances in her family to be more aligned with what she feels would be the greatest use of her resources carrying out her Divine Assignment, she looks for ways to live her Assignment at work and in volunteer organizations. She's not giving up on herself or her family, she's just waiting.

Your waiting period may be like Scott's:

> A little over two years ago, my position was eliminated from a company which I helped start. After recovering from the shock of losing my job, I started to listen to God's knocking on my heart telling me to start my own company.
>
> In listening to the constant knocking, I began a process of exploring what it was that God wanted me to do. It was during that exploration period that I discovered my Divine Assignment is to Promote Integrity, and I am to use my talents and skills in the computer engineering field to help small businesses, churches, and nonprofit companies.
>
> It took time. We waited. As months went by and the savings started drying up, I began to worry how I was to provide for my family. How would I put food on my children's plates, clothe them, and keep a roof over their heads?
>
> My company, Cornerstone Technologies, has just finished the strongest quarter we've ever had. But reflecting on the earlier times, along with the question "How has your Divine Assignment sustained you during times of transition?" I would say that *knowing* that God has a plan for my life, and even though I may not fully understand his plans, timing, or reasoning, it is comforting to know that I can fully rely on him. Was it easy? No. However, it has and continues to sustain me.

In the Mean Time...

Listening to a preacher deliver a sermon at the beginning of Advent season, I kept hearing him differently than what I know he intended to say. He was talking about the seasons of waiting we do in our lives, such as in between jobs or recovering from illness, and how we need to learn to live in the meantime—the period in between what is and what we want to be. While he was saying "meantime," I was thinking of all the people I've coached who feel like they're living more in the "mean time." The mean time is the period when it just doesn't seem fair, when we are grieving, when we are angry over a loss or an injustice, when we are feeling useless because of a diminished capacity, or our hands seem tied by circumstances.

Living in the mean time, or the meantime, is clearly evidenced by the life of Joseph. His story is detailed in Genesis 37–45. He indeed lived through some mean times as he moved through life fulfilling the hopes and dreams God had for him.

God's transformation of Joseph began with a dream. Joseph was given a dream that indicated he would be revered and important. He shared this dream with others who were, to say the least, offended by this revelation and sought to put him in his place.

The mean time for Joseph began with being tossed into a pit by his very own brothers. While they initially thought they would kill him, more compassionate heads prevailed and they decided on a less violent, more lucrative option for brother disposal. They sold him to slave traders. I'm sure Joseph was wondering about the meaning of his dream right about then.

He wound up in a rather cushy job, as slavery goes, as a servant in the house of Potiphar. Joseph continued to exhibit his regal character and won Potiphar's favor. Unfortunately, Mrs. Potiphar took a liking to Joseph in a way that wasn't so noble. After it became apparent to her that she wasn't going to get what she wanted from Joseph, she turned the sexual tables and framed him for attempted molestation. Joseph wound up in prison, again probably wondering about those now haunting dreams.

The mean time in prison found Joseph still being faithful to his gifts and character traits as he interpreted dreams for fellow prisoners. And his wisdom became apparent as his interpretations came true. The mean time in prison looked like it might be coming to an end as Pharaoh's cupbearer was sent back to the court to serve Pharaoh. Joseph's request to the cupbearer, "Remember me and show me kindness; mention me to Pharaoh and get me out of this prison" (Genesis 40:14), was forgotten, and the time seemed meaner than ever.

Remarkably one day the cupbearer's memory was refreshed when Pharaoh himself had troubling dreams. Joseph, still waiting in prison, was summoned. He used his gifts and displayed his character in ways that commanded Pharaoh's trust, and Joseph was put in charge of administration in Pharaoh's domain.

Now it's tempting to think that God's hopes and visions for Joseph were only evidenced in the position he ascended to as the right hand of Pharaoh. We have such a "success" mentality that we believe it's only when something noteworthy happens or when our lives have the fairy-tale circumstances that we are living out our Divine Assignments. But as we look closely at the story of Joseph, we see he lived out his Divine Assignment wherever he was. He was God's man in the pit, in Potiphar's house, in prison, and in the pinnacle of political power. His life is a powerful illustration of the understanding that our Divine Assignments are first about who we are, second about what we do.

Your mean time may involve a divorce, a creeping realization that your beloved parent is coming down with Alzheimer's, the emerging understanding that you were a victim of child abuse, waiting and holding your breath wondering how in the world a particular kid is going to turn out, or having to settle temporarily for a job when you really want an occupation or a career.

I don't suggest that you just need to buck up and put on a happy face when confronted with these challenges. I am saying that if you know your Divine Assignment and realize it is not dependent on your circumstances for you to carry it out, you will be able to draw from a deep well, a precious reservoir, that will help you understand that your life is not being wasted if all your resources and relationships are not being completely fulfilled.

Covenants Not Optional

One of the saddest things I hear people do with an emerging sense of personal purpose is dump their families. Believing we have heard a word from God, we may succumb to a prevailing mind-set of our culture—if this relationship isn't working for me or if you're getting in the way of my hopes and dreams, I can just leave you. One of the most rapidly expanding segments of people getting divorces these days is evangelical Christians. Some people get some sort of notion, some sort of "call" that is not initially supported by their spouses or children, and they think it's God's mandate to get rid of them. Discovering our Divine Assignments and recognizing the resources we like using best as we carry them out is *never* an excuse for getting out of a covenant relationship that we may be tired of or feel it doesn't suit us anymore.

I was at a CLASS conference one spring learning the ropes of being a Christian author and speaker from the masters, Florence and Marita Littauer. At that point in my life, I was starting to come out of the fog of being the mother of little children and getting fired up to "get my life back." I was beginning to get clearer glimpses of what I had always felt my life was to be about, but other things, internal and external, had gotten in the way. My kids were still little, but they were getting more to the age when I could look forward to the time they would be entering preschool. I would then have time to devote to writing and speaking, finally fulfilling what I believed my destiny to be.

Imagine my shock (and dismay) when Florence said, "And if you have small children at home, you need to raise them first before you go whole hog on the writing and speaking." But she was right. In having said yes to being a married woman and in agreeing to the covenant of motherhood by bearing children, I was first called to my family, to live my Divine Assignment fully with them first, then to turn my attention outward as family life shifted and changed with the ages and needs of my kids.

God doesn't call us to violate our covenants in favor of an alternative outlet for our Divine Assignments we have received. God will always call us to be patient and persistent partners with him, watching as the transformation in us triggers transformation in others. If we let our personal purpose overshadow our covenant relationships to the extent that we are breaking covenant, we are doing irreparable damage to all involved. There is a certain patience that needs to be exercised, especially if we're talking about a divorce for no other reason than creeping dissatisfaction. Almost all married couples experience times when they are tempted to be more interested in something (or someone) other than their spouses, and the number of marriages that end in a rather casual approach to divorce is astounding. This damage doesn't have to happen given a little time to get over and through predictable developmental bumps. Sixty-six percent of unhappily married adults who avoided divorce or separation reported being happily married five years later.[2]

When our loved ones seem to oppose a new appliance—a new interest or talent—we have discovered we feel called to explore as we are plugged into our Divine Assignment, it's usually because they don't see the vision we have seen, they don't fully understand how we intend to carry it out, and they may be concerned about what the new appliance will do to their own lives. People will not often be troubled by our responding to the call to be a more loving person, or to living our Divine Assignment of kindness, generosity, understanding, or some other benevolent mission we have been given. In fact, those closest to us may actually enjoy the renewed energy we have and the fruit of the Spirit emerging from living the Call for All more fully.

But when it comes to living specific dreams or responding to what we feel is a very distinct call of God on our lives to use a skill or passion more fully, oftentimes we may be talking about a change in job or career that may necessitate more schooling, leaving a financially comfortable position, or making a physical move. We may have a very strong sense that it's time to make adjustments that more fully align us with something very specific we feel we need to do.

I recall a specific moment in the clarification of how God wanted me to use my talents and skills to carry out my Divine Assignment. I had enjoyed the chance to get away for a weekend to spend time in reflection and life-direction exercises with one of the masters of this craft, Laurie Beth Jones. After two or three days of visioning, praying, and listening, I had a much better sense of where I was to be headed. I was feeling very happy about all of it while I was sitting by a quiet pool with a restful waterfall splashing in the background when all of a sudden a thought zagged across my mind as brightly and jaggedly as a bolt of lightning: "My husband is going to be scared to death."

I knew that before I went home to just dump this all over him, I would need to be clearer about some of the details such as timeline, financial possibilities and adjustments, evidence that this was possible, and a sense that I wasn't going to abandon my first covenants and responsibilities as wife and mother. Temptation raises its pious little head at a time like this and says, "Well, if your (husband, mother, children) just had more faith in God, they would support you in this." The truth is, our loved ones may have a great deal of faith in God, but they also want to see some forethought going into the process. When our call intimately intersects the lives of others, we need to exhibit the stewardship of our relationships. It's way too easy to get caught up in the fervor of a newly emerging call and forget the people around us. Having the

Call for All as a foundation, we know we might need to take some time merging what we envision with the realities of people around us. We may need some patience.

When our families protest our emerging direction, seek to remind us of our "priorities" and how much we're upsetting the family structure, or dismiss us almost immediately on financial grounds, usually what they are experiencing is fear. They are afraid they will be left behind. They are scared that we're not being financially responsible, and this will endanger a lifestyle they enjoy or hoped to enjoy. They may be fearful of change, of failure, of success, of living with a person of passion while they themselves don't have any. Whatever the protest may be, the root is often fear and uncertainty.

As the people proposing the change, we need to listen, to be respectful, and sometimes to wait for things to sink in. If this is the call of God and God wants it to get done, God will make the way clear. In the meantime, God may also be giving us ample opportunities to revel in and respond to his love, to learn to be more loving with ourselves, and to play well with others. Remember, we can live our two-word Divine Assignments anywhere, at any time, with anyone, even if we feel blocked from doing it with all of the tools and visions we possess.

But It's Summer Vacation

From the beginning of September to the end of May, I'm all business. I write, I teach, I coach. Since I'm an entrepreneur, my workday never really begins and never really ends. My kids are old enough that they are in school all day, and I give it my best shot to get all of my work done in the time they are gone. Some days it works; some days it doesn't.

During the school year, I help them stay on track, stay on top of the papers to be signed, drive to activities and performances, and do all the things a mom of two school-aged kids does. During the school year, I'm using the gifts, passion, and talents I've cultivated and chosen to use for the bulk of my working life. I believe I am making the best use of my highest gifts. I'm very focused, and I feel the power of living smack dab in the center of my Divine Assignment, which is to Stimulate Wisdom.

Then summer vacation hits. June, July, and August have a decidedly different rhythm. My kids are home with me, and the hours of lesson planning, researching, coaching with adults, and getting my thoughts and perspectives on paper evaporate into a whirlwind of going to the pool, crafting, hiking, chatting, keeping the peace, visiting the library, sightseeing, planning parties for their summer birthdays, and all of the other wonders of being the mom of two very active and very interested kids.

Candidly, I used to resent it.

Before I understood that my Divine Assignment was something I was given to carry out in any and all circumstances, situations, and relationships, I resented that I had to shelve the work life that gave me such a deep sense of accomplishment and peace. I felt like I was forced to unplug some of my precious appliances—some of the ways I lived my Divine Assignment—from my power source (God). I believed that only if I were exercising certain "gifts," in being productive and making an impact on the larger universe, was I truly living out my call. However, when I finally stopped to consider that my Divine Assignment, Stimulate Wisdom, could have a profound impact on my children, I realized that my worth, my purpose is validated anywhere, any time as I live what I was sent here to *be*, not what I thought I was sent here to *do*. I discovered a new, very important appliance—sphere of influence—for manifesting my power source!

Adjusting to how our Divine Assignments work out in our changing circumstances does seem to take a lot of practice, especially for women who have multiple roles, had children later in life, and have really enjoyed their careers. MaryAnn shared her struggle to stay centered in "the most wonderful time of the year"—the holidays:

> I'm still struggling with developing the discipline to focus on my Assignment with my family. Once again this year, despite my best efforts to pare down as many outside commitments (parties, concerts, etc.) as possible and to limit the decorating of our house to one very tiny tree, I have overwhelmed myself with Christmas preparations and expectations. I was a beast yesterday when everything seemed to be on my shoulders to make this Christmas complete. I'm working hard at saying no ("No, we can't take cookies to more than three neighbors," "No, I can't watch more than 30 minutes of my daughter's performance of 10 teddy bears dressed up and waiting for Santa even though it means she'll miss cookies and milk during intermission," "No, I can't be the one to do all the packing for our children"). I should have said no a lot more several weeks ago. I'm still learning how to apply my Divine Assignment in the family.

I completely love MaryAnn's candor on the challenges of applying one's Divine Assignment to the most intimate and everyday relationships. It may be relatively easy to exhibit our Divine Assignments with people we see periodically or with situations we don't encounter every day, but the rubber meets the road when the Divine Assignment impacts the way we tackle daily life.

Life Shifts

Having sold a whopping 250,000+ copies of *Transitions: Making Sense of Life's Changes,* William Bridges seems to have struck a nerve with the American culture. We obviously don't like the shake-up of having life unsettled, our expectations toppled, or our patterns broken.

Bridges says that, unlike what we believe is the normal cycle of things—beginning, middle, end—the life of a transition is actually end, middle, beginning. Something happens to signal the end of a relationship, job, lifestyle, or position. Then we go through the reorienting process to reassess who we are in the midst of it all and what we want as we move forward. The beginning is a time when we feel more in tune with life again. We don't feel "like our old self," because something about us has most certainly changed, yet we do have a sense of being reconnected to ourselves and our community.

Why is the notion of transition important to understanding our Divine Assignments? I fully expect that many of you picked up *Discovering Your Divine Assignment* because something just seems a little off in life. Maybe things aren't bad, but they're not as good as they once seemed to be and as you would ultimately like them to be. You might be in a transition. It might not be marked by anything as sudden as a deer hitting your car. It may simply feel like the wheels have been getting more and more wobbly on your car over a period of time. Discovering your Divine Assignment is a powerful piece of moving through your transition. To feel more connected to life and to get that deep-down sense of the essence of life, we need to embrace the Call for All. Uncovering and recognizing your Central Passion and your Greatest Strength may take you a long way toward pulling out of the mire of a long, slow, "I don't know where I'm going or why I'm here" transition.

Or you may have an excellent sense of where you're going or why you're here. You may be delighted by the work you've already done throughout this book. What you have uncovered is critical to weathering more jolting and unexpected transitions. William Bridges counsels that during the middle phase of a transition, when things may seem unbalanced and perhaps some of our normal and expected supports may no longer be available, we take this opportunity to discover what we really want.[3] Transitions often give us the much-needed, eye-opening experience that helps us, almost makes us, do the transformational work of sorting through the motives of why we use the various resources we use (see chapter 9). In transitions, we can use the grounded understanding we have of our Divine Assignments to realize that while we may not have the relationship or the job or the status to live our Divine Assignment as we once had, we have our Divine Assignment to steer us into the new relationships, jobs, or places in life. We can realize that our circumstances don't make our Divine Assignments, our Divine Assignments make our circumstances.

In the beautifully written book *The Modern Magi*, Carol Lynn Pearson introduces us to Annabelle Perkins, who lives in a small Midwestern town and works as a waitress. Annabelle has a heart condition, makes little money, and has one big dream.

Annabelle's beloved deceased mother left her a precious statue that Annabelle wants to take to the Holy Land during Christmastime to place at the birthplace of Christ. Her deeply devoted heart feels this would be the most wonderful gift she could give to express her love for Jesus.

To get to the Holy Land at Christmastime, she discovers, is going to take a year's worth of saving her extremely meager paychecks and tips. With her heart condition, she really can't work as much as she would like in order to earn the money more quickly.

Diligently and with her mission embedded in her heart, Annabelle saves enough money and is on her way to purchase her travel package. Oddly enough, she encounters a beloved family of customers at the restaurant just before she's going to visit the travel agency. She hears their story of a current distress. Then she hears the Voice. The Voice tells her, "You can give me my gift now."

Annabelle doesn't take her trip that year. And the same thing happens two more years after that one. Each time she hears the Voice saying, "You can give me my gift now." For three years running, Annabelle and Jesus change someone else's life with the money she has worked for so hard to save to give Jesus a gift she so desperately wants him to have.

Annabelle does ultimately end up taking a trip, but it's decidedly unlike the one she had intended to take. The trip God has for Annabelle is straight to the arms of Jesus where she can gain a full perspective on what he wanted from her—and wanted to give her—all along.

You might say God interrupted Annabelle on her quest to do something for him by doing something for her that brought her far closer to what she really wanted. Could it be that life interruptions are sometimes God interruptions trying to get our attention back on the true salvation of our lives?

Hidden in each of God's interruptions is something we may not always initially want, but is, in due course, God's greatest offering:

> The deep fear lying behind every loss is that we have been abandoned by the God who should have saved us. The transforming moment in Christian conversion comes when we realize that even God has left us. We then discover it was not God, but our image of God, that abandoned us. This frees us to discover more of the mystery of God than we knew. Only then is change possible.[4]

Has a deer smacked into your car lately? Where in your life do you, short-term or long-term, feel blocked from getting to live out your career dreams or full-life aspirations? Are there people and circumstances that keep you musing, "If only this weren't in my life, I could really be living out my purpose and what God really wants me to do—which, by the way, isn't this situation I find myself tending to." Don't give up on what you see or know to be in your future somewhere. Keep looking for the fruition of things you deeply feel God has called you to and given you a vision for. Find the beauty in the waiting or experience an unexpected unfolding of new visions, new relationships, new opportunities.

And remember the grounding truth that your Divine Assignment is given to you to live out wherever you are, whomever you're with. You can live your Divine Assignment even if you are all alone in the middle of a desert island, flat on your back with no discernable external resources. You will be able to affirm with Brother Lawrence:

> I possess God as tranquility in the bustle of my
>   kitchen...
> As if I were on my knees before the Blessed
>   Sacrament....
> It is not necessary to have great things to do.
> I turn my little omelet in the pan for the love of God....
> When I cannot do anything else, it is enough for me to
>   have lifted a straw from the earth for the love of
>   God.

Discovering More About Yourself

1. How has life not turned out the way you thought it would—for the better?

2. Where have you thought of your purpose in life as an occupation, career, or relationship? How would a change in one of those circumstances change your understanding of your purpose?

3. Have you been waiting to live a fuller expression of your gifts, talents, and interests? How can you carry out your Divine Assignment anyway?

4. Are you currently living in a "mean time," when situations and relationships are causing you pain and frustration? How could knowing and living the Call for All and your Divine Assignment help alleviate the situation? As with Joseph, what might the circumstances be preparing you for and for you?

5. What are your covenant relationships? How is God calling you to fulfill your Divine Assignment in each of them?

6. Are there times in your life when you have to unplug some of your preferred appliances to plug others in that don't seem as productive but are certainly as important?

7. When has God interrupted you? Are you still in the midst of the interruption? Has the interruption been resolved? What happened to your understanding of God's love for you?

8. Ask God what he wants you to make of the current interruption you're facing. Write his response.

❧

Dear God,

Things don't always turn out the way I hoped or planned. Sometimes this is a luscious surprise; sometimes it's shocking and unsettling.

God, thank you that you have given me the grounding of understanding the Call for All and my Divine Assignment. I can see that this will help me keep my balance when circumstances could throw me off.

And God, thank you that I have you with me in the midst of all the changes and transitions. You are my sole salvation. My Divine Assignment doesn't save me, but it's a tool to help me stay stable. My Divine Assignment doesn't keep me steady, but it's a resource you've given me by your grace to keep my bearings on you when the going is tough.

In Christ's name, amen.

What You'll Be Remembered For

❧

*Remember always that you have not only the right to become
an individual, you have an obligation to be one. You cannot make
any useful contribution in life unless you do this.*

ELEANOR ROOSEVELT

"When God asks, 'What will you be remembered for?'
what will you say?"

This question is one of 147 questions in a fabulous
little book by Richard Wilkins called *When God Asks…A Chance
to Change*. Richard experienced the opportunity to change
firsthand when he went from being a self-made millionaire to
being broke during a recession. He said in order to retain
some sanity, he began writing questions that eventually
became the book. He said of the book, "It changed my life,
not because I wrote it, but because I read it."

Discovering and living your Divine Assignment is all about
your character. Nothing will shape your character so powerfully as understanding that the God of the universe loves you
so intensely and intelligently that he has chosen you to be his
partner in bringing his kingdom to earth as it is in heaven.

Nothing will shape your character so powerfully as understanding that God's hope for you is that you will love yourself as he loves you. All else stems from the character that is shaped by these two realities.

What will your contribution be? One thing is certain. It will always be an outgrowth of who you are and what you decide to do with the resources God has given you to carry out your particular purpose.

If You Get Stuck

We started this book, way back in the introduction, with the opportunity for you to ask God a question. Maybe now God has a few for you.

I enthusiastically recommend Wilkins' book to you. And I suggest that when you get stuck in life, as we all do at times, you employ his formula for asking yourself questions about what you've learned from reading the book you have in your hands.

When God asks you, "What difference does it honestly make that I love you deeply, passionately, unconditionally, and eternally?" what will you say?

When God asks you, "Are you willing to love yourself as I love you?" what will you say?

When God asks you, "How's it going on the playground?" what will you say?

Becoming a healthy, real, and enthusiastic person takes honest conversation with God. Transformation will be a natural outgrowth of time and energy you invest in getting to know God and getting to know yourself. Both are worthwhile pursuits of the highest order! This kind of transformational process also "takes" best when you have someone to whom you are accountable. An insightful story from Russia tells of a priest who was walking along minding his own business when a royal guard stopped him at gunpoint. The guard demanded, "What is your name? Why are you here, and where are you going?"

The priest smiled wryly to himself and then at the soldier and asked, "How much do they pay you to do this work?"

The soldier, a bit surprised, replied, "Why, three kopeks a month."

"I'll pay you 30 kopeks a month if you will stop me every week and ask me these same questions," said the priest.

Don't do this alone.

The Beginning

Wow! You've done it! You have worked through the steps of discovering and beginning to live your Divine Assignment. Funny thing—you probably realize now more than ever that you are and always will be a work in process. That's as it should be, for if we ever got to the point where we felt we had every piece in place and knew exactly where and why we were here, if we ever got to the point where we felt we knew what the future held and what we were bringing to it, we would probably be more spiritually bankrupt than ever before.

That's the brilliance of God's plan for our lives. That's the beauty of his intention for our relationship with him. He never wants us to be so complacent or sure of the future that we don't need him. Being more in tune with God and his purpose for you is not so you will be comfortable; the transformation is so you will be filled with joy. There is a big difference in the discerning heart.

You do have a lot more clarity than when you started. You definitely have a toolbox from which to work as you continue to grow in grace and in wisdom. You have a strong foundation in the Call for All on which you can now erect the beautiful structure of your life's particular purpose with confidence that your contribution will be a deep gladness for you while you're filling a deep need in the world. You have much more discernment when it comes to choosing the best use for your gifts. You have some sorting techniques you can use when you feel like you're stuck. You can identify internal states that keep you from being all God hopes and envisions for you. You know that carrying out your Divine Assignment is never dependent on your external circumstances.

But most of all, you have the assurance that you are God's beloved child. God values and esteems you for who you are, not what you do for him or for anyone else. You are a vessel of grace to be filled over and over again only to be poured out in an endless supply just like the oil in the widow's jars (2 Kings 4:1-7).

❧

The best thing about the future
is that it only comes one day at a time.

ABRAHAM LINCOLN

A Note to Parents

❧

Nothing is so infectious as example.

FRANÇOIS DE LA ROCHEFOUCAULD

What do you want to be when you grow up?" is actually a fairly deceptive question. When we ask that of kids, we are usually trying to find out what profession they think they might enjoy. We're asking them what tasks they want to engage in on a regular basis or how they plan to make a living. Most of us would be shocked and feel like we had received an inadequate answer if the child replied, "I want to be a person who seeks and finds the goodness in myself and in others" or some other answer that focused on character. We think, *How are you going to make a name for yourself or make any money doing that?*

One of my fondest dreams is that every child would know, from a very early age, that they have worth and make a contribution simply because they "are." They are on this earth, right from the start, to change and impact their world just because they exist. Just think what would happen over the course of the next several generations if even a small percentage of parents started to focus on the Call for All for their children, then guided them to understand their individual Divine Assignments.

Sociologically, I can tell you we would see a marked decrease in teen sex and pregnancy, substance abuse, violence of all kinds, and suicide. All of these are often the results of kids feeling they aren't loved, aren't valued, and don't have a future.

As parents, we can help our kids immeasurably by paying attention to the fundamentals and playing to their particular strengths as we see them emerge. Doing both in combination is a terrific foundation for the advice the sage gives in Proverbs 22:6: "Point your kids in the right direction—when they're old they won't be lost" (MSG).

Giving our kids the direction and tools that come from the principles in this book will bring them health and comfort. The biblical notion of the "rod" has been somewhat misunderstood as a tool of punishment. Yet in the beloved Psalm 23, reference to the rod and staff are tools of guidance not punishment: "Your rod and your staff, they comfort me" (verse 4).

Why is helping a child with his Divine Assignment important to discipline? Studies show that kids who know where they're going are less inclined to use drugs or alcohol or to be involved in premarital sex. Two factors contribute to this healthier lifestyle: 1) they know and respect themselves, and 2) they believe they have value both now and in the future.

Why is knowing their Divine Assignments important to spiritual development? We're all always asking two basic questions: Who is God? Who am I? Divine Assignment discovery helps clarify both of these questions.

So what does it say to children about God that there is a plan? The very first thing God's plan communicates to kids is that God cares. God cares about them and has a reason for them being alive. God uses his amazing creative energy to bring them into being and holds the same kind of passion for their lives being lived to the fullest. Also, God having a plan for each of us tells us that God is very big. When you ask a child how many people there are on the face of the earth, then tell them that God has a plan for each and every person, and then point out that God wants to be actively involved in each of those plans running smoothly, a child can start to experience the immense expansiveness of God and his unique design for each one that completes the universal jigsaw puzzle

A third aspect this notion of a plan tells us is that God is creative. Only a very creative God could give each person such unique talents, such diverse interests, such distinct characteristics. God made funny people, artsy people, numbers people, people who can build bridges, raise families, and make clocks. And every creative thing we see another human being be or do is a reflection of a creative talent God has—God's got them all!

A fourth and very liberating trait we learn about God, when we realize that God has a Divine Assignment for each of us that starts with the Call for All, is that God is interested in faithfulness, not success.

The very first thing a child learns when he realizes he has a Divine Assignment is "I am important." The child realizes this because of how God feels about him. There are four questions children ask of themselves and of their worlds in their most formative years. The first one is "Do I matter?" Of course, very small children don't ask this out loud using those words, but they are constantly scanning the environment to see how others are responding to them. Even at early ages, we can tell them of God's love for them individually. We can help them love themselves by showing them how very loveable they are. We can even help them learn to "play well with others." That's God's basic plan for them.

What great fun to help children start exploring God's particular purpose for them—to start noting unique interests, character traits, and ways of doing things. As we reflect to them what we see and experience in them, letting them know that not everyone is like them, we can give them greater confidence that they are important, that they matter. And it's not just that they matter for the future, they matter now.

The second lesson kids pick up from understanding their Divine Assignments is "I am unique." Even from an early age, kids can begin to understand that they make contributions to the family and to the community that only they can make because they are the only ones of them we have.

Third, children learn "I am on purpose, not accidental." God has never once made a person and then said, "Oops, I didn't mean to do that." We can teach children beautiful verses from Scripture that reinforce God's intentional act of creating them. Share with them little bite-sized passages such as:

> Listen to me, you islands;
>   hear this, you distant nations:
> Before I was born the LORD called me;
>   from my birth he has made mention
>   of my name (Isaiah 49:1).

> I praise you because I am fearfully and
>   wonderfully made;
> Your works are wonderful,
>   I know that full well (Psalm 139:14).

> For we are God's workmanship,
>   created in Christ Jesus to do good works,
> which God prepared in advance
>   for us to do (Ephesians 2:10).

Let your children know that they have a particular purpose in this world. They were put on earth right where they are and precisely in this time in history to be who they are and to do what they do.

And last, when children appreciate the truth about God's Divine Assignment for them, they will know "I am not the sum of my achievements."

What is their Divine Assignment right now?

First, it's the three basics in the Call for All. How are we doing as parents to help our children love God? And what are we doing to help them love themselves? What activities are we teaching them when it comes to loving others?

Second, help them come up with a distinct Divine Assignment they can grasp to use this next week or month. Help your children understand that, while it is important and responsible to plan for the future, they have unique and exciting Divine Assignments from God right now. I like to play a game with my kids when we're in the car called "Which Do You Feel Is More Important?" I simply ask, "Do you think it's more important to be kind or to be fair?" or "Do you think it's more important to have a sense of humor or to be wise?" These questions make them think, and their answers give me clues concerning their Central Passions. You can also play a similar game with "What do you think you're good at?" using the words from appendix B (translated into kid-speak, of course).

The developmental phase in which discovering a Divine Assignment can be particularly helpful for your kids is high school through college. I have yet another dream when it comes to kids and this whole realm of particular purpose. I would love to walk onto any college or university campus in the country and hear the freshmen asking, "So what's your Divine Assignment?" rather than "So what's your major?" Telling people a major gives them a few clues about you, that is if your major is one you have chosen because it truly fits you and you're not living out the unlived life of your parents or have something else going on. But telling people your Divine Assignment gives them the clues they need to see what really makes you tick. When we help our high school and college students choose their courses in school and in life based on a Divine Assignment, we open up for them a huge array of really fun, exciting, and perhaps not-yet-thought-about choices for their careers. We also help them know that who they are is more important than what they do, but what they do is an important expression of who they are. We need to let kids know, especially in this culture where adults change entire career fields on the average of three times in their lives, that there are many ways for them to express their Divine Assignments. And that we are much more interested in faithfulness than success as defined by the world's standards.

Help your children understand that no matter what their circumstances might be, they can always make an impact by living their particular purpose. This is especially true if they have been through a divorce with you, faced the death of someone significant, moved, or any other transition that shakes their foundations.

Ultimately the best way for you to help your child understand and joyfully participate in this discovery is by living it yourself.

A Note to Pastors
and Church Leaders

❧

Love talked about can be easily turned aside,
but love demonstrated is irresistible.

W. STANLEY MOONEYHAM

*I*magine what your church would be like if everyone in your congregation knew their Divine Assignments and could find ways to match their Assignments with the mission and ministry options at your church! You would have a church full of on-fire people, and it could potentially cut the turnover rate in your membership.

A major challenge pastors and church leaders have is defining the Divine Assignment of their church and allowing that this assignment is what God has given them to do. The truth is most church leaders want their churches to be all things to all people, when the obvious reality is that different kinds of churches are necessary to meet the diverse needs of all kinds of human beings.

Of course, each and every church of Jesus Christ has the same ultimate mission, just as each and every individual is subject to the three elements of the Call for All. But what's

211

essentially going to ensure happy and productive church members is for your church to discover its unique "charisma" or spirit, its particular defining values, and its own articulated mission.

So what is the particular Divine Assignment of your church? Granted, it may be more than the two words suggested for individuals, since organizations are a bit more complex. But it shouldn't be too many more words, and certainly not more words than any person on the staff or in leadership can communicate when asked point blank what the mission of your particular church is. When you can articulate this, you will go a long way in being able to state your purpose in your promotional literature, in your bulletin, in your conversations with prospective members, and in the endless and various meetings that you and parishioners attend to keep things running in your corner of the vineyard. It will help your congregation in the same way it helps an individual. You will stay on track, stay true to purpose, and have a wonderful sense of the unique and remarkable contribution your church is to make in the kingdom of God.

I use three steps whenever I take a congregation through this process.

The first step is to get a clear definition of the congregation's Central Passion and Greatest Strength. A group of the church leaders, which includes paid professional staff and key lay leadership, spends a day with me working through the words which encompass these two elements and settle on a statement that most reflects what the leadership discerns to be God's particular call for this unique church. I then usually leave the scene for up to a couple months while the leadership hones what they believe to be true about their own particular fellowship.

The second step is one that groups seem to particularly enjoy. We set aside a Saturday and walk through the church with a specific set of questions, spending time in each of the key areas envisioning how their articulated particular purpose will be lived out in each of those areas and imagining how their particular purpose will be carried from each of those areas out into the community and into the world. It's a very exciting process and makes ministry come alive.

The third and final step is to prioritize the usage of the resources of time, talent, and treasure as a strategic, long-range planning function of the exercises.

Churches then have a clearer picture of what they are called to do, how the call will be lived out among the members and the community, and the timeline for implementation. The key to trying to get any organization to function effectively and with wise stewardship is to be crystal clear about the purpose of the organization.

A church in Indiana that went through this process did a very wise thing with the information it discerned in this process. The pastoral preaching staff each took a week in the pulpit to explain to the congregation what the particular Divine Assignment of their church meant to them and to the area of the ministry they served. What unfolded was a beautiful articulation to the congregation of what the distinct call of God on this particular church meant to its leaders. The leaders could share with the members a vision for the living of the mission within the church walls and beyond. People began to see their church actually moving in an intentional direction and knew more clearly how each of them could get on board and pitch in their own Divine Assignments for the good of the larger ministry that this deeply committed and richly resourced church could do in its community and beyond.

Knowing who you are and why you're here is deeply powerful for organizations as well as for individuals.

A Note to Employers
and People Managers

❧

*In my ideal world employees would know the mission statement
of the company they served, and all corporate executives
would know the mission statements of the people who serve them.
Each would complement the other.*

LAURIE BETH JONES

*I*t's no secret that the workplace and the workforce are much different today than just two or three decades ago. Employees move from job to job more frequently. Many new types of schedules and configurations are being implemented to try to accommodate the multiple roles that people are now trying to give equal attention. In fact, "one of the best predictors of retention for women is whether they sense that they can attend to a personal life and still develop in the company."[1]

The new workplace scene has developed a particularly interesting facet.

> Eighty percent of North Americans today say they would continue to work even if they won the lottery. Why? Because work has never been just about pay, and in a society relatively satiated with material goods, pay means even less. Study after study of

employee retention shows that while money is often
a factor in an employee's decision to leave, it is
rarely the primary reason. So we'll say it once more:
Knowing what *else* today's workers expect from work
is sure to keep your business competitive.[2]

Two of these emerging expectations identified by John Izzo
and Pam Winters in *Value Shift: The New Work Ethic and What It
Means for Business* are the expectation of work as a noble cause
and the expectation of personal growth and development.

Workers today want their businesses to have a deeper purpose than bottom-line profits. This is becoming increasingly
true of those who are just graduating from college. They feel
volunteer work is worthy of their time and making a contribution is important. Chances are excellent that those in the
workforce now are going to work longer hours doing more
complicated tasks than ever before. Their discretionary time
outside of work is severely limited. Therefore, they need and
want to feel that their work means something. Equally important, they want to feel their company or organization has the
same altruistic contributions through their products, their
sponsorships, and their meaningful interactions with the community. This is the expectation of work as a noble cause.

The second expectation, personal growth and development, is highly important to today's worker, especially the
younger ones who have a particularly low tolerance for
boredom. If they must do repetitive jobs, they need another
kind of stimulation to keep them interested in their jobs.
Good training in a variety of topics helps workers understand
that their employers really do care about them. "Among the
most popular life-management skills are leadership, financial
planning, retirement planning, stress management, creating
a work/family balance, and time management."[3]

Addressing these expectations has profound implications
as we talk about organizations and individuals discovering
their Divine Assignments. Your organization needs to be clear
about its Divine Assignment. Even secular organizations have

a heart and soul, and all that is created has been created by and through God (even if the organization doesn't recognize that). So there is a reason a company or organization exists that has deeper meaning than the profit dollar. Have you ever asked someone in a company why the company exists? If you can get him to give you something beyond a blank stare, many times an employee of a for-profit business will tell you about a product or a money-making service. For example, if you were to ask the manager of the local bookstore why his company exists, he may tell you "to sell books."

This is a perfectly fine answer on the surface, but it doesn't get to the true heart of core beliefs. Whenever I encounter this answer from an individual or a company, I ask a series of questions that all begin with "Why?" "Why do you sell books?" He might answer, "To make money." He might answer, "To get people to read." At that point, we're making a little headway, but we haven't hit the nerve quite yet. The trick is to keep asking "Why?" questions until you start to hover around something that looks similar to the words in appendix A.

Why is it important that an organization knows its Divine Assignment? Without this heart and foundation, over time there is a hollowness to the operation that doesn't inspire anyone. And in this new work culture, employees are looking for a match to their own interests, passions, and causes. For maximum employee retention, a company should be able to honestly tell potential employees what makes it tick in terms of core values to see if there's a fit. As Laurie Beth Jones counsels employees in *The Path*, "If your mission does not match or closely relate to the mission statement of the place where you are employed, prepare yourself for ulcers, sleepless nights, and countless hours of complaining (either by your boss, your co-workers, or your stomach)."[4] If the employee is hired and there is a nice fit, chances of a mutually satisfying and productive relationship are increased immensely.

The new cutting-edge, heads-up supervisor will be able to use a mismatched Divine Assignment as a potential diagnostic tool for troubled situations where an employee is obviously unhappy and not working to full capacity. If workers are looking for personal fulfillment on work time, what does this look like? "Countless studies boil it down to three variables: ability (the skills, experience, and knowledge that make a worker feel competent); values or preferred rewards (money, challenge, prestige, power or influence); and life interests.... Matching life and work interests is the most important of the three for long-term career satisfaction."[5] To use the language of the Divine Assignment, if an employer can meet the expectation of personal development in an employee by helping him know and understand his Divine Assignment and how it applies to what he is doing in his everyday work life, chances for employee satisfaction (which can translate into productivity) increase.

In preparing to give a workshop for a large metropolitan church, I was asked by the administrator, "This won't make any of my employees quit, will it?" He valued each of his employees and the contribution each of them made. I told him I couldn't make any promises on that count. However, in the course of the workshop and the processing the administrator did with each employee after they had discerned their Divine Assignments, he discovered that one of them really did have a deep yearning to be somewhere else on the planet making a significant contribution to another organization in another country. Over a period of a year or so, his employee finished her work in his church and headed overseas with the Peace Corps.

A few paragraphs ago, we saw the top topics for corporate training. All of them, without exception, are directly impacted by helping an employee discern and apply his or her Divine Assignment. What better gift could you give to your employees than helping them discover the root of what makes them tick, then showing them how it applies to every area of their lives, including their work life, in a powerful way.

If a company knows who it is and what it's about, it encourages its employees to do the same.

Central Passion List

Balance
Benevolence
Caring
Comfort
Compassion
Connection
Courage
Creativity
Devotion
Dignity
Faith
Faithfulness
Forgiveness
Freedom
Generosity
Gentleness

Goodness
Grace
Gratitude
Health
Honesty
Honor
Hope
Hospitality
Humor
Initiative
Joy
Justice
Kindness
Loyalty
Mercy
Patience

Peace
Perseverance
Purity
Reliability
Responsibility
Safety
Self-worth
Service
Simplicity
Trust
Understanding
Unity
Vitality
Wellness
Wholeness
Wisdom

Greatest Strength List

Accomplish
Achieve
Acknowledge
Actualize
Administer
Advance
Advocate
Affirm
Aid
Assess
Awaken
Believe
Bestow
Build
Call forth
Cause
Celebrate

Choose
Clarify
Communicate
Compel
Confirm
Construct
Continue
Counsel
Create
Defend
Deliver
Demonstrate
Describe
Design
Determine
Develop
Direct

Discover
Discuss
Dispense
Distribute
Educate
Embody
Empower
Enact
Encourage
Envision
Establish
Evaluate
Explain
Explore
Express
Facilitate
Finance

Find	Master	Relate
Formulate	Measure	Release
Further	Model	Remember
Gather	Mold	Renew
Generate	Monitor	Represent
Give	Motivate	Respect
Grow	Navigate	Restore
Help	Negotiate	Reveal
Highlight	Nourish	Safeguard
Host	Nurture	Save
Identify	Open	Seek
Ignite	Orchestrate	Share
Illuminate	Organize	Stand for
Illustrate	Perform	Stimulate
Impart	Plan	Strengthen
Improve	Plant	Summon
Increase	Practice	Supervise
Infuse	Preach	Support
Initiate	Prepare	Sustain
Inspire	Present	Teach
Integrate	Process	Translate
Invite	Produce	Trust
Keep	Promote	Uncover
Kindle	Protect	Understand
Know	Provide	Unify
Launch	Pursue	Uphold
Lead	Radiate	Utilize
Learn	Raise	Validate
Magnify	Reclaim	Value
Maintain	Recommend	Verbalize
Make	Refine	Verify
Manage	Reform	Welcome

NOTES

Introduction

1. C.S. Lewis, *The Great Divorce* (New York: Macmillan Publishing Co., Inc., 1977), p. 92.

Chapter 1—Unencumbered Enthusiasm!

1. Richard N. Bolles, *How to Find Your Mission in Life* (Berkeley, CA: Ten Speed Press, 2000), p. 11.

Chapter 2—God's Greatest Vision for You

1. Lewis Smedes, *My God and I: A Spiritual Memoir* (Grand Rapids: William B. Eerdmans Publishing, 2004), pp. 53-54.
2. Max Lucado, *God Came Near: Chronicles of the Christ* (Sisters, OR: Multnomah, 1986), p. 91.

Chapter 3—Am I Really Allowed to Do That?

1. Martin Luther King Jr., quoted in *Abounding Grace: An Anthology of Wisdom* (Kansas City, MO: Andrews McMeel Publishing, 2000), p. 197.
2. Charles Spurgeon, quoted in ibid., p. 160.
3. Parker Palmer, *Let Your Life Speak: Listening for the Voice of Vocation* (San Francisco: Jossey Bass, 2000), p. 41.

Chapter 4—Playground Rules for Life

1. Richard N. Bolles, *How to Find Your Mission in Life* (Berkeley, CA: Ten Speed Press, 2000), p. 43.

Chapter 5—The Personal Archeological Dig

1. Samuel E. Wood, Ellen Green Wood, Denise Boyd, *Mastering the World of Psychology* (Boston: Allen and Bacon, 2004), p. 325.
2. Julia Cameron, *Walking in This World: The Practical Art of Creativity* (New York: Tarcher/Putnam, 2002), p. 186.

Chapter 9—What's in Your Cupboard?

1. Samuel E. Wood, Ellen Green Wood, Denise Boyd, *Mastering the World of Psychology* (Boston: Allen and Bacon, 2004), pp. 323-24.
2. C.S. Lewis, *The Great Divorce* (New York: Macmillan Publishing Co., Inc., 1977), p. 79.
3. Neil Simon, quoted in *Abounding Grace: An Anthology of Wisdom* (Kansas City, MO: Andrews McMeel Publishing, 2000), p. 323.

Chapter 11—Who's Winning Your Mind Games?

1. M. Craig Barnes, *When God Interrupts* (Downer's Grove, IL: InterVarsity Press, 1996), p. 95.

Chapter 12—Life Interruptions or When the Deer Smacks Your Car

1. M. Craig Barnes, *When God Interrupts* (Downer's Grove, IL: InterVarsity Press, 1996), p. 9.
2. David Chaddock, *Children of Divorce: Can the Church Help Them?* (Indianapolis: Christian Theological Seminary, 2004), p. 147.
3. William Bridges, *Transitions: Making Sense of Life's Changes* (Reading, MA: Addison-Wesley Publishing Company, 1980), p. 124.
4. Barnes, *When God Interrupts*, p. 123.

A Note to Employers and People Managers

1. John Izzo and Pam Winters, *Values Shift: The New Work Ethic and What it Means for Business* (Toronto: Prentice Hall Canada, 2000), p. 60.
2. Ibid., p. 14.
3. Ibid., p. 117.
4. Ibid.
5. Laurie Beth Jones, *The Path: Creating Your Mission Statement for Work and Life* (New York: Hyperion, 1996), p. 68.

SUGGESTED READING

Barnes, M. Craig. *When God Interrupts: Finding New Life Through Unwanted Change.* Downer's Grove, IL: Intervarsity Press, 1996.

Bolles, Richard N. *How to Find Your Mission in Life.* Berkeley: Ten Speed Press. 2000.

Bridges, William. *Transitions: Making Sense of Life's Changes.* Reading, MA: Addison-Wesley Publishing Company, 1980.

Cameron, Julia. *Walking in This World: The Practical Art of Creativity.* New York: Tarcher/Putnam, 2002.

Guiness, Os. *The Call.* Nashville: Word Publishing, 1998.

Izzo, John B., Ph.D., and Pam Winters. *Values Shift: The New Work Ethic and What It Means for Business.* Toronto, Canada: Prentice Hall Canada, 2000.

Jones, Laurie Beth. *The Path: Creating Your Mission Statement for Work and Life.* New York: Hyperion, 1996.

Lewis, C.S. *The Great Divorce.* New York: Macmillan Publishing Co., Inc., 1977.

Lore, Nicholas. *The Pathfinder.* New York: Fireside, 1998.

Lucado, Max. *God Came Near: Chronicles of the Christ.* Sisters, OR: Multnomah, 1986.

Palmer, Parker. *Let Your Life Speak: Listening for the Voice of Vocation.* San Francisco: Jossey-Bass, 2000.

Pearson, Carol Lynn. *The Modern Magi.* New York: St. Martin's Press, 1994.

Peck, M. Scott, ed. *Abounding Grace: An Anthology of Wisdom.* Kansas City, MO: Andrews McMeel Publishing, 2000.

Ortberg, John. *If You Want to Walk on Water, You've Got to Get Out of the Boat.* Grand Rapids, MI: Zondervan, 2001.

Smedes, Lewis B. *My God and I: A Spiritual Memoir.* Grand Rapids, MI: William B. Eerdnams Publishing, 2004.

Wilkins, Richard. *When God Asks...A Chance to Change.* Nashville: Rutledge Hill Press, 2001.

RESOURCES FOR PERSONALITY ASSESSMENT

*P*ersonality assessment tools can be really fun to work with and can give you more insights into yourself. You can get a sense of what you prefer, what makes you tick, and what kinds of things and people you enjoy most. Assessments should be viewed as tools and not as prescriptive predictors of what you should do for a career or what you should think of yourself as a total package. Below are several websites you can go to for more information and access. There are fees attached to some of these tools. Have fun as you learn more about the wonder of you!

Keirsey Sorter, www.keirsey.com. This highly informative website will introduce you to four temperament styles—Artisans, Guardians, Idealists, and Rationals—and 16 types of personalities. The website gives you information on parenting and temperaments, dating and mating, and careers and jobs. You can take an initial sorting assessment that will tell you which temperament you are, then you can purchase additional analysis and information for $14.95.

Myers-Briggs Type Indicator (MBTI), www.personalitypathways.com. The MBTI is growing in popularity, especially in education and business. Similar to the Keirsey Sorter, the MBTI will give you one of sixteen personality typologies that you can use to assess who you are in your relationships, your career, your volunteer choices, and your leisure activities.

Path Elements Profile (P.E.P), www.lauriebethjones.com. From her book *The Path*, Laurie Beth Jones has developed an assessment that will tell you which of the four elements—Earth, Wind, Water, Fire—you're most like and what percentage of each you are. It's a fun, less clinical way to look at your personality. The cost is $55.

IPIP-NEO, www.personalitytest.net. This assessment tool is based on 70 years of research and development and measures what psychologist call "The Big Five." With this tool, you'll find out information on yourself based on five character traits—Openness to Experience, Conscientiousness, Extraversion, Agreeableness, and Neuroticism. Don't let the clinical terms put you off. This can give you some great insights into who you are. At the website, you can take the regular version of the assessment or a shortened version.

Enneagram, www.enneagraminstitute.com. This in-depth assessment helps you discover which of nine personality types you are—Reformer, Helper, Achiever, Individualist, Investigator, Loyalist, Enthusiast, Challenger, or Peacemaker. At the website you can take a free sample test, then pay $10 for an extended assessment.

If you would like to share how this book has helped you or if you'd like to consult with Robin individually or for a group or organization, contact her at:

yourwisdomtree@aol.com

or check out her website:

www.wisdomtreeresources.com

OTHER BOOKS BY ROBIN

Mom Overboard

Sink or swim. That's the decision facing many moms. Caught in nonstop activities for their kids and bombarded by myriad choices, moms are struggling—and feeling like they're drowning—every day.

Life counselor, personal coach, and busy mom Robin Chaddock offers 12 "Lifesavers" that will keep moms afloat and help them manage their lives.

Being a Wise Woman in a Wild World

What is wisdom in our topsy–turvy world? Professional success? Personal satisfaction? Becoming wonderful wives and mothers? Women who want to draw closer to God will be delighted by Robin's fresh insights into the pursuit and capture of wisdom as they become stronger women of God.